11·96

DIVINE DISCIPLINE

DIVINE DISCIPLINE

How to Develop and Maintain Self-Control

Rhonda Harrington Kelley

Foreword by Esther Burroughs

PELICAN PUBLISHING COMPANY
Gretna 1992

*The word "Pelican" and the depiction of a Pelican are
trademarks of Pelican Publishing Company, Inc., and are
registered in the U.S. Patent and Trademark Office.*

Library of Congress Cataloging-in-Publication Data

Kelley, Rhonda.
    Divine discipline : how to develop and maintain self-control /
Rhonda Harrington Kelley ; foreword by Esther Burroughs.
        p.   cm.
    Includes bibliographical references.
    ISBN 0-88289-892-2
    1. Self-control—Religious aspects—Christianity. 2. Discipline
—Religious aspects—Christianity. 3. Christian life—1960-
I. Title.
BV4677.D58K45   1992
241'.4—dc20   92-4576
                                                                         CIP

Unless otherwise indicated, all Scripture quotations are taken from
The Holy Bible: New International Version. Copyright © 1973, 1978,
1984 by the International Bible Society. Used by permission of
Zondervan Bible Publishers.

Scripture quotations marked NAS are taken from the *New American
Standard Bible.* Copyright © 1960, 1962, 1963, 1968, 1971, 1972,
1973, 1975, 1977 by The Lockman Foundation. Used by permission.

Scripture quotations marked RSV are taken from *The Revised
Standard Version of the Bible*, copyright © 1946, Old Testament section
copyright © 1952 by the Division of Christian Education of the
Churches of Christ in the United States of America and is used by
permission.

Scripture quotations marked KJV are taken from the *King James
Version* of the Bible.

Manufactured in the United States of America
Published by Pelican Publishing Company, Inc.
1101 Monroe Street, Gretna, Louisiana 70053

To my husband, Dr. Chuck Kelley, who has been a constant source of encouragement, love, and support throughout our eighteen years of marriage. His own self-discipline is an inspiration to me.

Contents

Foreword

I feel honored to call Rhonda my friend. I have observed her as a committee member, speaker, talk show host, teacher, speech therapist, and Christian sister. She is the essence of charm and grace. I am captivated when she is speaking. No one is more articulate. It's as if each word is chosen and caressed for the listening ear. Now, she has added "author" to her list of accomplishments, and you, dear reader, will be the richer.

The book you are now holding has traveled with me all over the United States, as I disciplined myself to write this foreword. Am I ever glad I did! From beginning to end, I found help on every page, and just the help I needed in my own personal life.

What I liked best is the way Rhonda keeps pointing the reader to the Word of God. Then she gets practical, real-life applications. You will not get the feeling that she has come to these convictions easily, but rather through struggle, hard work, and discipline. She has discovered that true freedom is a by-product of "dedicated discipline." You will be glad she helps you learn the process of self-discipline.

This book will help today's woman to build self-control into her life, coming under the power of the Holy Spirit to live a godly life. I enthusiastically recommend this book!

ESTHER BURROUGHS

9

Acknowledgments

It is appropriate for me to begin my acknowledgments with praise to the Lord for His guidance and strength in the task of writing this book. This message came from God, Who first convicted me about my own lack of self-control. He then helped me develop divine discipline so I could share my experience with others. The Holy Spirit has inspired my words as I have written this book. To God be the glory, great things He hath done!

I also want to express deep appreciation to my husband, Dr. Charles "Chuck" Kelley, for his unconditional love, constant support, and invaluable assistance. His theological insights and technical advice were a great help in this project, as they are in any responsibility I undertake.

A special thank you to several family members and friends who gave of their time to proof this manuscript. Many of them allowed me to share some of our personal experiences. A special thanks to several friends whose second homes provided productive work weeks.

I am grateful for the hundreds of Christian women who have heard this message at conferences, retreats, and luncheons. Their expressed needs prompted me to write this book, and their positive comments keep me disciplined in life. May God continue to use what He has taught me to change others.

Finally, I want to thank Pelican Publishing Company for their support and assistance in writing this book. I am grateful for the

Christian testimonies of the owners, Dr. and Mrs. Milburn Calhoun, and I am particularly appreciative for the professional help of my editors, Nina Kooij and Jimmy Peacock. I sincerely enjoyed working with them.

Introduction

Well, Rhonda, you can do it! It was about two years ago now when I became convicted that it *had to be done*. I finally decided I could do it. No, I actually became convinced that *God could do it through me*.

I am like many people, perhaps including you, who appear on the outside to be "in control" while on the inside are "out of control." Yes, I have always seemed to my friends to be organized and disciplined. Well, I am organized and in control in many ways. But only the Lord and I knew that there were areas of my life out of control.

Of course, at times everyone feels utterly, totally helpless, and uncontrolled. I, too, must confess to this feeling. There are times when I give in to impulses and later regret my actions. But God was not speaking to me about momentary behaviors. He spoke to me about a greater need—*the need to be disciplined in myself*, the need for discipline of my very being.

Several years ago as I prepared to teach a Bible study on the fruit of the Holy Spirit from Galatians 5, God began to do a great work in my life. At first I was intimidated by the last of the nine virtues called temperance or self-control. Who in her right mind would want to teach others about a topic so personal and revealing? But I endeavored to begin a systematic study, never realizing that *God would convict me and change me*.

I began to learn that self-control is the crowning fruit of the

Spirit and that, without self-control, a Christian cannot enjoy the other eight precious blessings. I did so want to experience love, joy, peace, patience, kindness, goodness, faithfulness, and gentleness, but I learned that I cannot have any of these without self-control. God convicted me of the need to have self-control in order to be an obedient, maturing believer who can enjoy the fruit of Christ-likeness.

At first I didn't realize that God wanted to deal with me about self-control. My biggest concern was overeating and weight control. You see, over the years, I had added some pounds. I was expert with excuses such as: "I'll start watching what I eat on Monday." "I'm big-boned and I carry my weight well." "You can't live in New Orleans and be on a diet." In fact, I had tried every fad diet known to man! As is usually the case, the pounds I lost quickly found their way back. But God had a new diet plan for me. His plan was fail-proof. He promised success from the very start.

Now this book is not a diet book. Nor does it offer a quick-fix for a lifetime of overeating. (If that is your only purpose in reading it, you'll be disappointed!) But, instead, I am sharing from my personal experience the lessons God taught me in self-discipline. For God used my concern about my weight to force me to deal with the far more important issue of self-discipline. As I focused my eyes on Him, and not on losing weight, I learned that I could claim His power to gain control over all areas of my life. God didn't want me to be skinny; He wanted me to be satisfied, happy, and at peace in every area of my life. To my surprise, as I began to gain victories in the war for self-control, the battle of weight control was won along the way.

While I am hesitant to write these words (you see, your reading means more accountability for my self-discipline), I trust that *God will speak to you personally* and convict you of the need for more discipline in your life.

Let me quickly tell you about the joy before you become overwhelmed by the sacrificial commitment. As I learned about Spirit-controlled self-discipline, I grew in my spiritual life in a way never experienced before. I became more disciplined in all areas of my life. And guess what? I lost fifty-five pounds. So the Lord gave me the extra blessing of a smaller body as a reward for my personal discipline and spiritual maturity.

Please keep reading—and even rereading. Allow God to use my personal journey toward spiritual discipline to encourage you. You, too, will learn that *there is great reward in leading a disciplined life*.

RHONDA HARRINGTON KELLEY

DIVINE DISCIPLINE

CHAPTER 1

A Harvest of Righteousness
(Discipline: Why Is It Important?)

No discipline seems pleasant at the time, but painful. Later on, however, it produces a *harvest of righteousness and peace* for those who have been trained by it (Hebrews 12:11).

Has this ever happened to you? While sitting in a lovely restaurant, a mother and child enter. The child is beautiful — long flowing blonde hair gathered back in a ribbon, dressed in a bright floral print with matching shoes and purse. However, as time passes, your impression of the precious little girl changes as she misbehaves, becoming loud and disagreeable. You realize that this young child has no self-control. The embarrassed mother has no control over her unruly daughter. What an impact on you and other patrons in the restaurant. What an impact on the child! This little girl, though beautiful in appearance, will be hindered in life both personally and socially by her undisciplined behavior.

Discipline must be taught to children by their parents. Through loving parental discipline, a child learns self-discipline and self-control. Our heavenly Father wants to teach His children self-control. Contrary to popular belief, abundant love does not make discipline unnecessary. Instead, it is because of deep love and concern that parents discipline their children and teach them self-discipline. *Discipline of self is not caught; it is taught.* While some people seem naturally to have more willpower, all of us must develop self-discipline in order to lead more productive, happy, fulfilling lives.

It is an undisciplined world in which we live! Few people today are in control of themselves. Most people have adopted the attitude: "If it feels good, do it." Rarely do we consider the long-term effects of our actions. Rarely do we try to control our impulses in order to change our behavior through self-discipline. As Christians we are challenged to be in control of all areas of our lives. Our human natures are carnal and of the flesh, while our spiritual natures should be righteous and holy. In fact, as Christians we should be disciplined in all areas of life — physical, mental, social, and spiritual.

Self-discipline is necessary in our personal lives and in our relationships with others. Without discipline, we cannot grow and mature. Without discipline, we cannot experience the fullness of God. Without discipline, we cannot minister to others. Since we do not want to fail in our Christian walk, we must learn self-discipline. Discipline is necessary for personal development, for spiritual growth, and for Christian service.

Personal Development

Professional athletes must be disciplined in their daily lives. In order to excel in their endeavors, personal commitment and faithful practice are required. It is usually the most disciplined athlete who wins the competition. Discipline demands sacrifice and pain. It is not easy to awaken early each morning to exercise, to train all day, to plan strategy at night, and to delay social life. But dedication and discipline pay off in the end. Many rewards of a disciplined life are invisible to the human eye, but other rewards are earthly symbols of the crowns of glory to come.

In her book, *All That Was Ever Ours*, Elisabeth Elliot discusses the reward of a disciplined athlete. While freedom and discipline have come to be regarded as mutually exclusive, freedom, in fact, is the final reward of discipline. Freedom is to be bought with the high price of self-discipline, not merely claimed. The professional athlete is free to perform in competition only because he has been

> . . . subjected to countless hours of grueling work, rigidly prescribed, and faithfully carried out. Men are free to soar into space because they have willingly confined themselves in a tiny capsule designed and produced by highly trained scientists and craftsmen, have meticulously followed instructions and submitted themselves to rules which others defined (page 61).

It is only with dedicated discipline that freedom is found.

Recently, I read a newspaper article about an Olympic figure skater named Brian Boitano. The caption read, "Boitano Counts His Blessings." This young champion described his unique method of coping with the pressures of an exhausting practice schedule, frequent skating exhibitions, and grueling travel. He stated that when these demands become overwhelming, he simply "pauses and counts his blessings." He certainly has many blessings to count! He has won gold medals in international competition and Emmy awards for television performances. His self-discipline has been rewarded with professional accomplishments. Brian Boitano discovered that freedom is not the absence of restraints. *Freedom results from the practice of necessary disciplines.*

Development of personal character requires self-discipline in all areas of life. Discipline is necessary for health and fitness. Discipline is essential for financial stability and professional stature. For the married, discipline is needed for building relationships with spouse and children. For all Christians, discipline is the foundation for moral excellence and personal ethics. *Self-discipline is the process; personal development is the product.*

The area of my life requiring the most discipline is physical fitness. I have started many exercise programs, but have had great difficulty maintaining my commitment to them. Initially, I am enthusiastic and faithful. But, in time, I become disinterested and inconsistent. Other activities soon take priority. If I am disciplined in my physical life, then I will receive the rewards of personal accomplishment as well as health and vitality.

Jesus Himself grew in personal character. It is recorded in the Gospels that "Jesus grew in wisdom and stature, and in favor with God and men" (Luke 2:52). God demonstrated to us in the life of His own Son the importance of personal growth. As Jesus grew in size and matured in age, He also increased in knowledge and in wisdom, both in the eyes of God His Father and of humanity. In fact, one New Testament translation says "he kept increasing" (NAS) in these attributes. As believers, we are to keep growing in our personal life as well as in our relationship to the Lord.

The Apostle Paul encouraged his friend Timothy to be disciplined in his personal life as well as in his spiritual life. In 1 Timothy 4:7,8 Paul wrote to his young disciple, "Discipline yourself for the purpose of godliness; for bodily discipline is only of little profit, but godliness is profitable for all things, since it holds promise for the present life and also for the life to come" (NAS). For Paul, disciplined speech and conduct were a reflection of one's personal faith and a defense against immorality.

My husband and I had an opportunity to practice character building while we worked simultaneously on dissertations. Doctoral studies alone are intense, but writing a dissertation is the most difficult part of the process. Extensive research, endless writing and rewriting, and the dread of defending our work before a panel of experts brought tremendous pressure to our personal lives and relationship. Although abandoning the project would have made our lives easier, it would also have prevented us from attaining our educational and professional goals. Living with the restraints imposed by our academic programs drew us closer together as husband and wife and helped us complete our tasks. Without this experience in self-discipline and perseverance, we would not have the ministries God has given us today.

Many of our friends think it is a miracle we survived the stresses of that experience. However, we both saw it as a time of building up, not breaking down. There was significant growth in our personal characters. We now depend daily on those qualities we developed then — sacrifice, perseverance, and hope. The sacrifice of time and leisure activities was worth the reward of graduation. Besides that, when we speak together before a group, people enjoy introducing us as a "paradox" (pair-of-docs)!

The development of personal character requires discipline. It is not easy to keep on growing. It is much easier to be content in our present state. But God tells us to continue growing. So, discipline is necessary for personal development as well as for spiritual growth and Christian service.

Spiritual Growth

Spiritually mature Christians will admit that their spiritual growth did not come easily. In fact, giants of the faith will relate the sacrifice and self-discipline necessary for growing in Christ. Talk to any of your spiritual heroes, and they will describe the daily discipline and selfless sacrifice of their spiritual pilgrimage.

Gordon MacDonald, in his book, *Rebuilding Your Broken World*, wrote about the price of regular discipline. "Spiritual discipline is to the inner spirit what physical conditioning is to the body. The unconditioned athlete, no matter how naturally talented, cannot win a world-class race" (page 199). The undisciplined Christian, no matter how sincere, cannot live a Spirit-filled life. Self-discipline is necessary for spiritual growth and abundant life.

Preparing to teach a Bible study requires discipline. It also ensures personal spiritual growth. Several years ago, I taught a student wives' course entitled "Spiritual Disciplines" at the New Orleans Baptist Theological Seminary. The students were required to keep a daily prayer journal which encouraged the development of spiritual discipline. I told them of the joy they would receive through the discipline of recording prayers and answers to prayer. I quickly realized, however, that I needed to "practice what I preach." So I resumed a daily prayer journal, a practice I continue to this day. An activity which began as an assignment soon became a habit which resulted in holiness. Such joy and peace is mine as I exert personal discipline in my spiritual life! I can truly enjoy the fruit of the Spirit!

Paul lists the fruit of the Holy Spirit in Galatians 5:22,23. These nine virtues are to be sought by a growing Christian. Along with love, joy, and peace, the apostle includes self-control as an evidence of the Christian life. Many biblical scholars would say that self-control is the last or crowning fruit of the Spirit. Without self-control, a believer cannot experience all the blessings of the Spirit. Self-discipline then is an important part of spiritual growth and maturity.

In his book, *Celebration of Discipline*, Richard J. Foster concludes that while grace is a free gift of God, followers of Christ must pay a high price to grow in grace. Christians must sacrifice the time necessary to study the Bible, to pray to the Father, to witness to others, and to minister to the needy. This personal sacrifice of time and energy results in spiritual development. Spiritual discipline is for a definite purpose — spiritual growth.

In 2 Peter 1:4-11, Simon Peter challenges all believers to grow in their faith. He reminds us that God's precious promises cannot be claimed without acts of faith. Among the qualities of righteousness, Peter includes self-control:

> For this very reason, make every effort to add to your faith goodness; and to goodness, knowledge; and to knowledge, self-control; and to self-control, perseverance; and to perseverance, godliness; and to godliness, brotherly kindness; and to brotherly kindness, love. For if you possess these qualities in increasing measure, they will keep you from being ineffective and unproductive in your knowledge of our Lord Jesus Christ. But if anyone does not have them, he is nearsighted and blind, and has forgotten that he has been cleansed from his past sins (2 Peter 1:5-9).

Self-control is a grace gift from God — a quality God promises us as we experience His Spirit within us. In order to receive this gift of discipline from God, we must grow in faith — diligently increasing in wisdom and knowledge. Self-control for the believer comes by steadfast faith and spiritual growth. Peter follows his mention of self-control with a challenge for perseverance. Certainly, we must persevere in our discipline. To decide to be self-controlled is one thing — but to keep on being self-controlled is another matter. God wants us to persevere in self-control.

In his letter, Simon Peter gives us the bottom line concerning self-control and the other godly virtues. Without them, he says, we are useless, unfruitful, blind, short-sighted, and unclean. With them, however, Peter says that we are useful, fruitful, keen-sighted, and clean. The believer who practices self-control "will never stumble" (2 Peter 1:10 NAS). I want to be the kind of believer who never stumbles, don't you?

Recently, in an evening worship service at All Soul's Church in London, I repeated with the congregation a prayer of confession. The prayer concluded with the importance of a godly, righteous, and disciplined life.

> Almighty and most merciful Father,
> we have strayed from your ways like lost sheep.
> We have followed too much our own ways and the
> desires of our own hearts.
> We have broken your holy laws.
> We have failed to do what we ought to have done;
> we have done what we ought not to have done; and
> we cannot save ourselves.
> Yet, Lord, have mercy upon us helpless sinners.
> Spare those, O God, who confess their faults.

Restore those who are penitent, according to your
promises declared to all men by Jesus Christ our Lord.
And grant, O most merciful Father, for his sake, that
from now on we may live a godly, righteous and
disciplined life, to the glory of your holy name.
Amen.

Those words reminded me that righteousness and self-discipline as well as confession of sin are essential to Christian growth.

The spiritual growth of an individual believer is in great part dependent upon persistent discipline in the areas of prayer, Bible study, evangelism, missions, and service. Without self-control, a Christian fails to grow spiritually. Without persistent self-control, a child of God is disobedient and discouraged. Spiritual growth and personal development are not the only reasons for a Christian to be disciplined. It is impossible to minister effectively without self-discipline.

Christian Service

Discipline is essential for personal development and spiritual growth. However, did you know that self-discipline is also a prerequisite for Christian service? The demands of busy schedules force us to discipline our time in order to minister. But God's Word also cites self-control as a necessary qualification for service.

In his instructions concerning spiritual leaders, Paul discusses the attributes of a pastor, of deacons, and even of deacons' wives. The "overseer" or pastor of a church is to be "the husband of but one wife, *temperate, self-controlled*, respectable, hospitable, able to teach" (1 Timothy 3:2). Likewise, deacons are to be controlled in their personal life. They are to be men of high standing and great faith. Paul also instructs that deacons' wives "are to be women worthy of respect, not malicious talkers but *temperate* and trustworthy in everything" (1 Timothy 3:11). Paul concludes that self-control is not only a quality of godly character, but a qualification for Christian service.

Discipline of self seems in New Testament letters to be a personal trait essential to church leadership. How often do we examine the self-discipline of a candidate for church office? We should ask an individual being considered for spiritual leadership about his or her ability to control outward and inward behaviors through the power of the Holy Spirit. Or, at the very least, we should observe this godly quality in an individual before entrusting spiritual leadership to him/her.

On one occasion, I had the privilege of serving on our church nominating committee. Our task was to recommend to the church the names of members who were qualified for leadership in particular areas of church life. Without exception, all of us agreed that one individual was truly qualified to teach Sunday School. I quickly volunteered to call the person, whom I had long admired for her godly character. She had always appeared to be self-disciplined in her personal life. I was both surprised and pleased at her response when I asked her to consider teaching an adult Bible class. She answered with confidence and kindness, "Teaching is not a priority in my life now. God has other things for me to do. But I will pray for you as you seek God's choice to teach the class." Her response reminded me of the importance of self-control in Christian service. Because she had determined her priorities in ministry, she declined any distraction from those priorities. Personal discipline is not only a godly virtue, but an essential part of discovering God's plan for one's life and ministry.

Any Christian desiring to be an instrument of the Lord must examine his or her self-discipline. Without self-control, a Christian is a vessel unfit for Christian service. Lack of determination can detour one from God's will. A lack of discipline in personal or spiritual life leads to failure in ministry. The Bible records the life stories of many people who were unfit for service due to their poor self-control.

Though greatly gifted by God, Samson lost his strength, his freedom, his eyesight, his dignity, and his life because of lack of self-control (Judges 16:17-21,30,31). Moses, the leader of the Hebrew people, lost his opportunity to enter the Promised Land due to his faltering discipline (Numbers 20:1-13). Eve's poor self-control meant the loss of her home (the beautiful garden of Eden) and the penalty of sin for her children (Genesis 3). Lot's wife lost her very life when she could not keep herself from looking back on the destruction of Sodom and Gomorrah (Genesis 19:24-26). Their lack of self-control resulted in loss of privilege on earth and loss of usefulness for eternity.

What a great price we pay for a lack of discipline! What a great loss we suffer! Self-control is necessary to a believer for personal development, spiritual growth, and Christian service. Without self-control, a Christian is unable to build character, uninterested in spiritual maturity, and unwilling to serve others. God needs His children to be disciplined so they will be fit vessels for His service.

Disciplined Christian service is required by all obedient believers. Jesus Christ is our perfect role model of a servant. If we desire to be like Christ, we must be servants. As Charles Swindoll wrote in his book, *Improving Your Serve*: "Since Jesus Christ, the Son of God, took upon Himself the role of a servant, so must we. The One who could have been or done anything, consciously and voluntarily, chose to be one who served, one who gave" (page 211). We must discipline ourselves to serve others unselfishly just as Christ served.

The development of self-discipline was necessary for my personal spiritual growth and personal maturity. God demonstrated that His power is substantial while my power is weak. He helped me grow spiritually in a way I've never grown before. I saw myself as a weak individual, an immature Christian who was weak in her own power. But God showed me that as His child I had access to His infinite, supernatural power, even in the mundane events of life.

God taught me that He wants to help me gain control of all areas of my life — even the daily, unconscious acts such as eating. He assured me of the temporal and eternal rewards of a disciplined life. After all, who doesn't want to look better, feel better, and act better? But the more important and lasting truth is that self-discipline yields eternal rewards experienced not only on earth, but in heaven. *God has the power to help you gain control of your life!*

BIBLICAL STUDY

Read 2 Peter 1:4-11 in several translations of the Bible. List below the words Peter uses to describe God's promises to and qualities for the Christian who is seeking self-control.

Promises   *Qualities*

PERSONAL APPLICATION

1. Examine your personal character. Do you need to develop a more controlled, godly life? List here several personal traits you desire to possess and then determine to claim them.

2. What is your spiritual temperature? Are you "on fire for God" or "lukewarm in your faith"? Decide on your first step toward spiritual maturity. Write your commitment below then pray that God will empower you to be consistent in prayer, Bible study, witnessing, and ministry.

3. If a church nominating committee was searching for church leaders who were temperate and self-controlled, would you qualify? In what ways has your Christian service been limited by your lack of discipline? Be honest with yourself as you commit your ways to the Lord.

Dear Lord,
Convict us today of the need for self-discipline in order to develop personally, to grow spiritually, and to serve faithfully.

Amen.

CHAPTER 2

A Heart of Restraint
(Discipline: What Is It?)

But the fruit of the Spirit is love, joy, peace, patience, kindness, goodness, faithfulness, gentleness and *self-control*. Against such things there is no law (Galatians 5:22,23).

During one of their daily telephone conversations, Mary confessed to her dear friend Joan that she was frustrated with herself because she had no willpower! She had tried unsuccessfully for months to lose those ten pounds and just couldn't. In a somewhat jealous outburst she cried, "You have so much self-control. You have never been overweight."

In the next few minutes Joan explained to her distraught friend that while she had no problem with her weight, she, too, struggled with poor self-control. With three small children and a busy schedule, Joan just never seemed to get anything done. "I have no willpower when it comes to housework or daily chores. I put off everything until tomorrow; then it all builds up and overwhelms me. I wish I had some self-control. But I don't know anyone who has it — and, in fact, I don't even know what self-control is!" Mary and Joan were both in serious need of help, but first they needed to discover the true meaning of self-control.

Self-control has different meanings to different people. For many of us, the consequences of its absence are so painful we seldom think about what it is. It has an impact in all areas of life, though it is not a virtue easily recognized or defined in an individual. So then, what do we mean by self-control and self-discipline? Let's look at the meaning of this term from a variety of perspectives.

31

A Dictionary Definition

Most modern dictionaries classify the word "self-control" as a noun, a thing to be described. According to Webster, self-control is "the ability to restrain one's impulses or expressions of emotion." Another popular dictionary says that self-control is "control exercised over oneself or one's own emotions, desires, actions, etc." The Collins dictionary and thesaurus define self-control as "the ability to exercise restraint or control over one's feelings, emotions, reactions, etc."

One fact is certain — self-control is a behavior. According to the experts, behaviors are learned responses. If that is true, there is hope for us all, for behaviors can be changed by deliberate action and reaction. These definitions also reveal that self-control can be exercised only by the individual to restrain his own impulses or feelings. An unspoken assumption is that everyone has uncontrolled emotions, desires, and actions which need training. Self-control is more than a matter of temperament. It is a characteristic or behavior which can be developed!

As a speech pathologist, I work daily with children who need to change a disordered behavior. Most of my patients have speech problems. Speech is a behavior which can be changed. It is my task to identify the impaired behavior, to set realistic goals for changing the behavior, to develop a treatment plan to pursue those objectives, and to observe the results of the altered behavior. The goals often cannot be met if the child is unable to assist in the process. He must try to improve his behavior. Self-control is a necessary prerequisite for behavior changes.

Familiar synonyms for the word "self-control" include self-discipline, self-mastery, and self-restraint. The most popular expression today is willpower. It is common to hear someone bemoan a personal lack of control as poor willpower. Each of these words refers to the ability to control one's own feelings and behavior.

A better understanding of the term "discipline" or "self-discipline" is also important to our study. Discipline is generally defined as the training or conditions that develop improvement or restraint in physical or mental powers. *Discipline requires training, and training demands systematic obedience.* Self-discipline further implies the act of training one's own feelings, desires, and actions. Self-discipline leads to self-control. However, these terms are most often used interchangeably to mean personal restraint or willpower.

A Biblical Understanding

God's Word talks often about self-control in both the Old and New Testaments. But, what do the scriptures mean by "self-control"? What does the original text actually say to explain the term?

The actual word "self-control" is not used in Old Testament scriptures, though its characteristics are described. In the book of Psalms, David speaks of the control of his outward behaviors and his inner thoughts. David's plea is that his own impulses will be godly and righteous: "May the words of my mouth and the meditation of my heart be pleasing in your sight, O Lord, my Rock and my Redeemer" (Psalm 19:14). Again in Psalm 24:3-5, David describes the necessary qualities for holiness:

> Who may ascend the hill of the Lord? Who may stand in his holy place? He who has clean hands and a pure heart, who does not lift up his soul to an idol or swear by what is false. He will receive blessing from the Lord and vindication from God his Savior.

Purity of heart and hands could only come to David through self-control.

In the New Testament, the actual word translated as self-control occurs often. The frequently used Greek word *egkrateia*, meaning "the virtue of one who masters his desires and passions, especially his sensual appetites" (*Unger's Bible Dictionary*), has numerous New Testament references. In Galatians 5:23, 1 Corinthians 9:25, 1 Timothy 3:2, and Titus 1:8, a form of *egkrateia* is used in the Greek text. Each time the Greek word is translated as self-control or temperance.

I began my study of self-control by reading the scriptures. First, I found the references in several Bible concordances under the headings "temperance" and "self-control." There were many scriptures cited. As I read each passage, I read the surrounding context and other cross-references. I learned so much from my personal Bible study. Then, I read what others had to say about self-control in commentaries and in other books. God gradually led me to a biblical understanding of the concept of self-control that had practical application.

The scriptures teach that self-control, or temperance, is a virtue of the Christian life essential for spiritual maturity. Self-control or godly restraint is included with the fruit of the Holy Spirit and in the qualifications for church leadership. Paul values self-control in all believers. Without self-control, the other blessings of the Spirit cannot be experienced. He describes self-control as the control of one's entire life under the direction and will of God as expressed in a life totally submitted to Christ in all areas. *Self-control then is an outward sign of inward growth.*

When I first read Paul's description of the fruit of the Spirit, I must have overlooked the last one. Love, joy, and peace were such obvious virtues. Patience, kindness, and goodness were definite traits to be desired. Faithfulness and gentleness were also godly characteristics. But self-control seemed out of place in that list of blessings. God taught me through Paul that self-control is the essential ingredient for all the fruit of the Spirit. Without self-control, the other fruit cannot be experienced.

Imagine making a chocolate cake and leaving out an important ingredient — the flour, the baking powder, the sugar. What a disaster! You could not enjoy the flavor of the butter or the sugar without the main ingredient. As a Christian, you cannot enjoy the fruit of the Holy Spirit without self-control. Paul the apostle was convinced of the necessity of self-discipline.

My mother knows that my husband, Chuck, loves cornbread. There was a time early in our marriage when three times in a row she forgot an important ingredient in the cornbread. It became a family joke. The first time she forgot the baking powder; the cornbread was flat. The second time she didn't use the right amount of oil; the cornbread stuck to the pan. The third time the cornbread looked beautiful — but she had forgotten the salt; it had no flavor. Cornbread without all its ingredients, in accurate measurements, is not good cornbread. Without self-control, there is no abundant life! Self-control is an essential ingredient for joyful Christian living. (By the way, my mother has finally succeeded with her delicious cornbread!)

Dallas Willard, in his thought-provoking book, *The Spirit of the Disciplines*, discussed Paul's repeated emphasis on self-control. Self-control was a "constant drumbeat in his life and writings" (page 102). For Paul, the controlled life is obtained only by extensive discipline. Paul mentions self-control at least five times in the first two chapters of the book of Titus alone. Other writers of the New Testament agree that self-control is an essential virtue of the Christian life.

A Theological Perspective

Many theologians have studied the ideal of self-control. Commentaries expound on its meaning, particularly in discussions about Galatians 5, 2 Peter 1, and 1 Timothy 3. These insights are worthy of our brief consideration.

In his commentary on the book of Galatians, biblical scholar William Hendriksen explains that "self-control is the power to keep oneself in check" (page 225). All of us need a system of checks and balances. In the same way that our forefathers designed our nation to work justly under a system of checks and balances, so God has created each of us with the ability to cross-check our own behaviors. Self-control then is the checks and balances system within — the means by which we recognize our sins of omission and commission and redirect our behavior.

According to seminary professor Dr. J. Terry Young in his book about the fruit of the Holy Spirit, "Self-control is the expression of the mature life which has learned to walk with God in perfect obedience" (page 118). Self-control requires total surrender of every thought in obedience to Christ. This practice not only results in changed behavior but in a changed heart! Self-control then denotes spiritual maturity in a Christian whose actions and attitudes have been changed by the Holy Spirit.

A pastor once told his congregation that "self-control is the believer's wall of defense against his inner man." That visual image helps me understand what is meant by self-control. As we develop personal discipline, we actually erect a wall or shield around our lives, protecting us from our own sinful desires. This barrier of self-control becomes our internal strength as well as external protection. Self-control must be solid and stable in order to withstand the evil forces within and without us. Internally, we receive the power and courage to fight evil forces. Externally, we receive the strength and stamina to defend our Christian values.

Castles have always been intriguing to me — not just because of the wealth and power they represent, but because of the strength and protection they provide. I love to visit old castles in England. Windsor Castle, Warwick Castle, Sudeley Castle, and countless others are encircled by tall, thick walls of stone. Those walls were built to defend the inhabitants within from enemies without and to stabilize the military forces inside to counteract their opponents outside. Self-control erects a wall around us, giving us inner strength and outer protection. Without that barrier, our lives are vulnerable to the archenemy of the Christian, Satan.

Other expositors explain self-control, or the power to take hold of passions, as the control of one's entire life under the direction of the will of God. Self-control is one of the essential fruit of the Holy Spirit. Where the Holy Spirit is active in a believer's life, there will be self-control. In its broadest sense, then, self-control is the mastery over all evil tendencies and the commitment to a godly manner of living. It is the fruit or product of the Holy Spirit's ministry to the individual believer.

Further understanding of self-control comes from a study of the uncontrolled lifestyle. Scripture declares that self-control is opposed to debauchery, gluttony, lust, drunkenness, gossip, outbursts of temper, envy, and strife. In fact, even good things (such as work, play, and money) in excess can be wrong. Prior to his discussion of the fruit of the Spirit in Galatians 5, Paul describes the works of the flesh. The deeds of the flesh include: "sexual immorality, impurity and debauchery; idolatry and witchcraft; hatred, discord, jealousy, fits of rage, selfish ambition, dissensions, factions and envy; drunkenness, orgies, and the like" (Galatians 5:19-21).

A follower of Christ cannot be ruled by fleshly desires and walk fully in the Spirit. Self-control will be accompanied by the other fruit of the Spirit. A lack of self-control will be accompanied by the fruit of worldliness. The issue of self-control is not a neutral issue. Without self-control, we will be conformed to the world. With self-control, we will be transformed into the likeness of Christ (Romans 12:2).

In Acts 24, Paul rebuked Felix, the corrupt governor of Syria, who had stolen Drusilla from her husband. Paul challenged the governor's immorality and lack of self-control. The apostle spoke of righteousness and temperance as evidences of faith in Jesus Christ. Felix became so frightened by this pronouncement that he sent Paul away. As a result of his poor self-control, Felix hardened his heart, lost his rule, and left Paul imprisoned in Rome. His experience demonstrated the pain and loss of an uncontrolled life.

There may be times in your life as a Christian when God calls you to stand firm in your faith. At that time, it will be easier to yield to your instinct of self-preservation and ignore your call to self-control. God tells you to turn from your flesh and to His Spirit for power. Don't abandon self-control as Felix did, but persevere in self-control as Paul did. As a result you will not suffer the consequences that befell Felix, but will savor the fruit of the Spirit that Paul enjoyed.

The scriptures teach and theologians emphasize the grave importance of self-discipline in the Christian life. A study of God's Word clarifies the meaning of self-control and motivates its practice. Self-control is a godly virtue to be developed by all believers who walk in the Spirit. It is more than a matter of human discipline. It is a reflection of a close personal relationship with the Holy Spirit.

A Personal Reflection

My own study of the fruit of the Holy Spirit helped me to understand better the meaning of self-control. As sinful beings by nature, none of us has control of individual ungodly impulses or evil thoughts. Even when we sincerely attempt to exercise control of our deeds and desires, we fail. Self-control is not an automatic response or a natural behavior for believers. Instead, we readily develop a pattern of undisciplined, unacceptable behavior and uncontrolled, ungodly passions.

Self-control has never been a favorite word for me. But, as God began to reveal the true meaning of this Christian virtue, and as I came to understand its full meaning and intent, I began to appreciate the word. God convicted me of my need to pursue diligently discipline in my life — not only to battle the evil temptations of the world, but to battle my own sinful, uncontrolled nature. That task at first seemed overwhelming, but later it became possible — with the help of God.

Specifically, in my "battle of the bulge," God helped me to control my eating. Self-control meant saying no to chocolate and yes to fresh fruit. Self-control meant smaller portions and no second servings. Self-control meant ignoring cravings and focusing on

Jesus. While changing my food habits was not easy and eating healthy food was not always satisfying, my personal discipline plus God's power resulted in self-control of my eating.

For the Christian, there is hope! While we believers alone are unable to develop sufficient control of our desires and passions, God can help us to be disciplined. Where your own power fails, God's supernatural power succeeds! Therefore, a believer should define self-control as "Spirit-control" — the discipline of oneself through the power of the Holy Spirit. In this lesson, I learned the true meaning of self-control and found hope to master it. *Divine discipline is Spirit-controlled discipline of oneself!* It is not something with which we are born — it is something God wants to teach us. Divine discipline is behavior He taught me and it is a virtue He wants to teach you!

BIBLICAL STUDY

Study the scriptures to understand better the biblical meaning of the term "self-control." Find the following references in your Bible, underline them, and note any cross-references as you study God's teaching about self-control.

Psalm 24:3-5

Galatians 5:22,23

Titus 2:11-14

Write your own definition of self-control based on your biblical understanding.

PERSONAL APPLICATION

1. Attempt to understand better the general meaning of the word "self-control." Ask several people to explain their knowledge of self-control. Then look up the definition of self-control in a dictionary. Record what you have learned in the space below.

2. Find a New Testament commentary on Galatians and read the section on Galatians 5. What does the biblical scholar have to say about self-control? What new insight did you receive from the writer's perspective?

3. What is your own understanding of self-control? Have your thoughts changed since reading the Bible and discussing your ideas? Write here your own definition of self-control. Develop a statement of your commitment to Spirit-controlled self-discipline.

Dear Lord,
Help me understand what You mean by self-control so I may seek Your power to pursue it. Give me the knowledge from Your Word and the wisdom of others to develop this virtue of restraint.
Amen

CHAPTER 3

The Disciplined Lifestyle
(Discipline of What? Outward Behaviors)

If a man cleanses himself . . . he will be an instrument for noble purposes, made holy, useful to the Master and prepared to do any good work (2 Timothy 2:21).

Overeating — extravagant spending — vicious gossiping — releasing of anger — these are all evidences of an uncontrolled life. Ungodly behavior usually indicates a lack of inward discipline. Many different inappropriate behaviors result from poor self-control. Which of your outward behaviors give evidence of your inner weakness?

Ron has always had a weight problem. He frequently loses weight, but he quickly gains it back.

Sue is always broke. She cannot resist a sale, and she cannot control her spending. The mall is her downfall.

Linda has a biting tongue. She is quick to snap back a harsh response and to circulate vicious gossip. Her words are painful and cruel.

John regularly loses his temper — at home, at work, and even at church. Without warning, he yells and becomes upset, often about trivial things.

These examples include only a few outward manifestations of poor self-discipline. At this point, let's search the scriptures and study human nature for ways in which poor self-control will hinder our own lives and our personal relationships. Scripture encourages us to control our outward behavior so we can be holy instruments to do God's work (2 Timothy 2:21).

In a discussion of the disciplines of outward behavior, let's examine both ungodly actions and godly practices. Each of our lives will be marked by visible behavior — those actions seen by the world. Which behaviors will mark your life — ungodly actions or godly practices? As Christians we must strive to coordinate the desires of our hearts with the demonstrations of our human behavior. It is essential for Christ-like individuals to avoid unrighteousness, to engage in holiness, and to purpose for godliness.

Avoid Unrighteousness

One of life's greatest challenges is controlling the evil desires of our human natures. We are born with a sinful nature. Look at any small child, and you will know he does not have to be taught to do evil. Misbehavior comes very naturally!

A young child quickly learns what is right or wrong in the eyes of his parents. However, when given the chance, the child will "test the waters." Parents see it every day. There is a natural tendency to try to get away with wrongdoing without suffering the penalty.

My father-in-law loves to tell the story of the testing of his authority by one of his young grandsons. Perry was told by Papa not to open the refrigerator. However, strong-willed Perry pulled a chair over to the refrigerator under the watchful eye of Papa. For about thirty minutes, these two engaged in a battle of the wills as Perry with hand on the refrigerator door stared at Papa sitting at the kitchen table. Papa's eyes spoke volumes to his grandson who by nature was defiant. Perry wasn't taught to resist authority; he was born with a rebellious nature. All of us have an inborn sinful nature.

Perry finally became discouraged and left the field of confrontation. Papa, in his steadfast authority, had won this battle of the wills. This would not, however, be the last battle. You see, all of us, God's children, constantly challenge authority — especially God's authority over our lives. We must, therefore, be disciplined in our outward behavior if we are to be like Christ.

Think about the behaviors you have a difficult time controlling. Are they behaviors that bring glory to God, that make you more Christ-like, or that build up others? Peel away the layers. At the bottom you will find that behind those behaviors resistant to self-control is a desire to continue a behavior you know God wants you to stop. The theological concept expressing that desire is "sin." Poor self-control is simply a symptom. Sin is the cause of rebellion against God.

Christians are to avoid unrighteousness. Our society accepts certain ungodly behavior and encourages other unacceptable action. Behaviors once shunned by parents are now sanctioned by their children. As Christians, we must obey God's law and seek His direction in *all* our ways. The question is not, What can I do and still get to Heaven? but, rather, Is there anything in my life God wants to control? Are there any outward behaviors in my life that hinder my witness in the world?

My mother grew up in a small town in central Alabama. While her mother and siblings were faithful church members, her father never attended church. He was always a good man — moral, honest, and generous. He expressed a belief in Jesus, but he had no interest in church. As a young child who loved the Lord and regularly attended services, I innocently asked my grandfather why he didn't go to church. His response had a profound impact on me. Over the years, he said, he had watched the church members and even the preachers. Their lives had been no different from his. And many of them, in fact, seemed dishonest and immoral. He felt no need to attend church since it seemed to make little difference in the lives of many of those who attended regularly. The world sees an inconsistent life as hypocritical. The unrighteous outward behavior of a Christian can be a stumbling block to the unbeliever.

Christian adults must control their own behavior, and concerned parents must teach their children to be disciplined. During my teenage years, my Christian parents tried to instill in me a desire to be holy and godly in my behavior. At times that was a real challenge for them! New Orleans wasn't an easy city in which to rear children. Truly Christ-like Christians were few. In fact, I had only one real Christian friend in my high school. However, the fervent prayers and wise instruction of my parents helped me learn some self-control, even as a sometimes rebellious teen.

One memorable conversation with my dad comes to mind. My father handed me a Bible as I was walking out on a date. Though he laughed, he seemed serious as he said, "Put this New Testament on the front seat between you. He will have a hard time jumping over Matthew, Mark, Luke, and John." In his own way, my dad was trying to encourage me to avoid unrighteousness and to engage in godly conduct.

The book of James speaks to believers about immoral behavior.

James instructed Christians to live a godly life in the midst of a pagan world. In the third chapter, the New Testament writer spoke about Christian ethics and ungodly character:

> We all stumble in many ways. If anyone is never at fault in what he says, he is a perfect man, able to keep his whole body in check (James 3:2).

It is, therefore, understood that all of us will sin, because no one is perfect but Jesus.

Later in that same chapter, James spoke specifically about the sins of the tongue. Many of us need to control what we say, to tame our tongue. Words are powerful. They can be used to build up or to destroy another person. The same mouth that praises God can curse another person made in God's image. We must all carefully *examine the words of our mouths* which are outward expressions of our inward thoughts. Don't let gossip or slander demonstrate to others your lack of self-control. Avoid the temptation to spread rumors or perpetuate half-truths. Your speech is an outward behavior that needs to be controlled.

Paul, in his writings to the Christian church, gave much attention to all the sins of the flesh. In fact, he included a plea for purity in each of his letters. Galatians 5 lists the various outward acts of the sinful nature in relationship to God, man, and self. The sins against God include idolatry and witchcraft — worshipping other gods or other spirits. The sins against man include hatred, discord, jealousy, fits of rage, selfish ambition, dissensions, factions, and envy. Even Christian behavior often evidences hate, jealousy, selfishness, and envy. The sins against self include substance abuse and sexual immorality. God teaches us to abstain from evil doings — to avoid unrighteousness.

There are many evidences of poor self-control in our outward behavior. Gail MacDonald mentions several symptoms of what she calls "the unsharpened life" in her book, *Keep Climbing* (pages 121-124). Poor mouth control, ungodly peer standards, excessive whininess or self-pity, overinvestment in tasks and short-changed relationships, inner deceit, and disobedience to the laws of God are six signs of a life that needs spiritual sharpening. These ungodly acts hurt the individual and many other loved ones. Self-discipline is needed for spiritual sharpening.

From a psychological perspective, the excesses and abuse in behavior can result in disorders of self-control. Psychologists frequently counsel individuals with specific compulsive behaviors including profanity, obesity, gambling, shoplifting, pornography, and drinking. These inappropriate social behaviors evidence the universal consequences of poor self-control. Extreme problems of self-control often require professional counseling if the individual is to regain control of his disordered behavior.

In my work as a speech pathologist, I have had many opportunities to treat children who suffer from autism, a developmental disorder which produces severe communication problems. Most autistic individuals are unable to control their inappropriate social behaviors such as flapping their arms, spinning around, or smelling objects. Actually, they often seem comforted by these peculiar behaviors.

Perhaps you saw the movie *Rainman*, starring Dustin Hoffman as an autistic adult. The actor vividly portrayed the unusual ritualistic behaviors of autism which make it so difficult for autistic people to function normally in society. His inflexible daily schedule included watching his favorite television program at 5:00 P.M. While traveling with his brother, he insisted on stopping at the house of strangers to demand the use of their television to watch his show. His inappropriate behavior frightened people but satisfied his need for routine. He was unable to control his actions or to conform to society. While this example may be extreme, all of us are at times unable to control our behavior.

The practice of self-control comes through discipline of actions and behaviors as well as attitudes and feelings. Self-control comes with Christian maturity which must be demonstrated in a godly life. A Christian must be pure in the eyes of God and man. Self-control is necessary in our relationships with others. Discipline of our outward behavior serves our long-term interests as well as those of others.

Engage in Holiness

Not only must a Christian avoid unrighteousness, but a disciplined Christian will engage in holiness. Many good people act in a godly manner, but only God's people are godly! As we mature in Christ, we act like Christ. Our outward behavior includes personal spiritual growth and faithful service. To be truly Christ-like, we must eliminate ungodly behavior. We must evidence a holy life.

A disciplined Christian makes time for God! No matter how busy or how mature, a growing believer spends time daily with the Lord. Disciplined daily devotional time leads to self-control in outward behaviors and inward desires. Lack of time with the Father opens the door for disobedience and misbehavior. A believer must protect himself or herself from unrighteousness by engaging in holiness.

Spiritual discipline is essential in the areas of prayer, Bible study, witness, and service. It is important to be involved in public worship and praise in addition to personal prayer and study. All followers of Christ are commanded to be active in their faith daily. *Faith falters when faith isn't flourishing!*

My father had been in full-time evangelism for many years when his unpracticed faith allowed him to falter. After years away from the Lord, my dad is finding his spiritual foundation and his evangelistic ministry is being rebuilt by God. He has returned to the basic spiritual disciplines and spends hours daily in personal prayer and Bible study. He is renewing his relationship with the Lord as he prepares himself for a new, more effective ministry. His message to Christians now is, "Don't take your eyes off Jesus! Don't leave your first love! Do whatever it takes to spend time daily with Jesus." A good life and ministry to others is not enough to promote spiritual growth. We must maintain and develop our personal relationship with the Lord through spiritual discipline.

In what areas are you undisciplined spiritually? It is important for us to identify our own weaknesses in order to grow stronger. Dallas Willard in *The Spirit of the Disciplines* said, "The need for extensive practice of a given discipline is an indication of our weakness, not our strength. We can even lay it down as a rule of thumb that if it is easy for us to engage in a certain discipline, we probably don't need to practice it" (page 138). What spiritual discipline is the most difficult for you to practice regularly? Chances are, God wants you to be more disciplined in that area.

The verses in 1 Corinthians 8:2,3 speak to us directly about spiritual growth. In this passage Paul told the Corinthian church that "the man who thinks he knows something does not yet know as he ought to know. But the man who loves God is known by God." As immature Christians, we know nothing. As maturing Christians, we learn many things but only as we spend time with God. Time alone with the Lord does not come easily. However, it is only through discipline that we are able to grow in faith and engage in holiness.

Recently I read an article in a family magazine about self-control for young mothers. Some very practical tips were given for mothers who "feel like screaming when life seems out of control." The advice was sound but incomplete. Certainly, it is helpful to be organized and flexible as well as to have a sense of humor and to keep balance in life. But the article failed to mention that a mother who is personally disciplined in her own spiritual life will have extra help at her disposal — God's supernatural power to bring control to some of life's most uncontrolled situations.

The prophet Isaiah wrote of the Lord, "You will keep in perfect peace him whose mind is steadfast, because he trusts in you" (Isaiah 26:3). When we focus on ourselves, we will always see at least the shadow of inadequacy. We are finite and human, always lacking something. God is infinite and eternal, never lacking anything. We can know that checks drawn on His account will never bounce. When we have the self-discipline to give Him control, God empowers us.

In my professional life, I have often felt divine power to handle difficult situations. Many times I realized it was my spiritual walk that prepared me for the unexpected encounter. I am committed to my morning prayer times that undergird and strengthen me for the unknown challenges of the day.

In the medical setting where I work, I frequently interact with very opinionated professionals. I remember one experience that caught me off guard. A physician confronted me about a patient. He failed to understand my work with the child. Though initially startled, I gained my composure and confidently explained my treatment plan. He immediately seemed to understand, and then thanked me for my explanation. I did not realize the pressure that had built up inside of me. When I went to the bathroom later, I was surprised when I began to cry uncontrollably. God had given me the strength to control my emotions in the midst of the situation. I am grateful that my day had begun with prayer and that God had equipped me to meet a surprise challenge.

God's power often helps us control our outward behaviors. I thank God that instead of stress I have His strength when I engage in holiness — pursuing a daily walk with Him. When I look into His face, I know I can find the strength to maintain self-control. The practice of spiritual discipline can help the believer avoid unrighteousness, engage in holiness, and purpose for godliness.

Purpose for Godliness

A disciplined lifestyle demands daily self-control. Self-control is necessary in regulating our hearts' desires and our physical actions. Our outward behavior must exclude ungodly actions and include holy living. Resistance to temptation and the practice of spiritual discipline develop self-control. It is also essential to purpose for godliness — to determine to live a life committed to God.

Each of us must develop a definite purpose in life. How often do you examine your life's purpose? I'm not speaking here about your activities or priorities. Instead, your life's purpose should be your life's direction, the focus which sets the boundaries or limits of all your activities. What is your present purpose in life?

At the beginning of each new year, I reassess the goals and objectives for my life. I actually make a list of my long-term and short-term goals spiritually, physically, mentally, and socially. Making a list of the things I plan to accomplish is not as hard as writing a one-sentence statement of my life's purpose. As a Christian, my activities may change, but my life's purpose should never change. My purpose in life should be to do the will of God. Self-control is needed to focus on that purpose and keep it central to all that I do.

Last year I listed several specific goals under each of the following categories: personal, spiritual, marriage, family, ministry, and career. I have worked hard this year to accomplish these goals. And, it does take work! However, again I struggled with writing my life's purpose in one sentence. After many attempts, I settled on this statement of my overall purpose in life: "With God's help, I will continue to grow spiritually and personally as I minister and witness in His power." That statement of purpose has directed the activities of my life. Self-control has been necessary for me to fulfil that purpose.

Self-discipline must be exerted in order to purpose for godliness. The Christian's supreme sacrifice in self-control is to give herself to someone else. For the believer, the one to whom she gives herself is God revealed through the Holy Spirit. The Christian life calls for a daily commitment and discipline. *Self-sacrifice through self-control is necessary for self-fulfillment.*

A precious example of selfless sacrifice comes to my mind. One of the young girls with whom I worked at church was asked to buy a present for a needy child at Christmas. Her family was sharing a food basket and some gifts with an impoverished family. After going to the store with her few dollars, the little girl returned home empty-handed. She decided to give away her favorite doll — the one possession she treasured most. This unselfish child knew that her special friend would love her doll. So she truly gave of herself. Christ expects this personal sacrifice from all His children.

O. Henry wrote a lovely story about a young couple who had little to give each other at Christmas time. The loving wife cut her hair and sold it in order to buy a chain for her beloved's pocket watch. Her husband sold his prized timepiece to buy a beautiful set of silver combs for his wife's hair. Both gave all they had for each other. God seeks our dearest sacrifice, and this sacrifice requires our self-control.

To the Philippians, Paul wrote, "I press on toward the goal to win the prize for which God has called me heavenward in Christ Jesus" (Philippians 3:14). The Apostle Paul was a man with a single purpose. His only focus in life was to know God. He accomplished many things and he engaged in many activities, but he steadfastly maintained a single purpose. Our goal in life is to know God. If we remain disciplined through daily self-control and devotion, then we will receive the prize — eternal life with Christ. *Our purpose is discipline; our prize is heaven.*

Discipline is required daily. Life offers us many opportunities and choices. Often we must say no to some good things in order to say yes to the best things. We may not prefer the best things at first, but they may be essential to our Christian growth. It is important to choose those activities that complement our purpose in life. We can do so with the help of the Holy Spirit. A natural result of self-control is the presence of the Holy Spirit in us.

Richard J. Foster gives several principles for controlling outward behavior in his book, *Celebration of Discipline* (pages 90-95). He challenges us to consider carefully our actions as we make daily decisions.

His principles can help us to avoid unrighteousness, to engage in holiness, and to purpose for godliness:

1. Buy things for their usefulness rather than their status. If you need it, buy it. Don't buy it because it looks good to others.

2. Reject anything that is producing an addiction in you. Limit yourself in activities or practices that can become habit-forming.

3. Develop a habit of giving things away. When you have no further use for something, give it away or share it with another.

4. Refuse to be propagandized by the custodians of modern gadgetry. Timesaving devices usually cost more but rarely save time. Invest in the original, do-it-yourself models.

5. Learn to enjoy things without owning them. Many things in life can be enjoyed without owning them if we control our spending.

6. Develop a deeper appreciation for the creation. Enjoy God's beautiful world as you control your excesses.

7. Look with a healthy skepticism at all "buy now, pay later" schemes. Don't allow yourself to become in debt and under the control of others.

8. Obey Jesus' instructions about plain, honest speech. Be truthful and dependable in your communication with others.

9. Reject anything that breeds the oppression of others. Don't exploit others through your own selfish ambitions.

10. Shun anything that distracts you from seeking first the kingdom of God. Try to focus on your spiritual journey.

These sound principles will promote self-control in your lifestyle.

Biblical guidelines should be used to help us control our actions. Our outward behaviors reveal our inward spirit. Society would have us minimize our actions and maximize our attitudes. In reality, we find that both are important. A great deception in the practice of Christianity today is the idea that all that really matters is our internal feelings, ideas, beliefs, and intentions. That notion is untrue, because we are body *and* soul. We are both doing and feeling. We must be disciplined outwardly and inwardly.

In my own personal pilgrimage, I have found it easier to control my outward behaviors than my thoughts, desires, and feelings. My mother taught me to watch what I say and do. (Sometimes I have trouble doing that!) But I learned quickly that no one can control my thoughts but me. While I may inhibit my actions to be more appropriate and acceptable, my feelings may be uncontrolled. I may not say, "I really don't like you," but I often think that — and more.

Frequently, I have trouble controlling my thoughts. I will confess now to only one of many instances. For several years, the secretary at my office was a real "thorn in my flesh." She had many little habits which irritated me. Her most offensive behavior was her note writing, daily reminders with red underlining and exclamation marks. While this practice may have helped others, it unnerved me because I was very organized and was fully aware of the report which needed dictation. With God's power, I was able to hold my tongue and keep from telling her of my frustration (though I admit I often told my colleagues of my disgust). On one occasion, I truly lost control and wrote back to her in red ink with underlining and exclamation marks. It is somewhat easier to control our actions than our feelings.

Concerning the control of my eating, I found those same tendencies to be true. It was much easier for me to exercise self-control in what I ate and how much I ate than in my thoughts about food. While eating steamed broccoli or fresh fruit, I could still think about potatoes au gratin and chocolate eclairs. My thoughts were a greater challenge to control. But, the same God Who can help me behave in a godly way can help me think godly thoughts.

My prayer changed! I prayed that God would teach me self-control of both my actions and my thoughts. I committed my desires and feelings to Him as well as my life and works. For me, it was a control in my body and soul — a control in doing and feeling — a control outwardly and inwardly.

Now that we have discussed the discipline of outward behavior, let's look next at the discipline of inward behavior. God would have us examine our hearts as well as our hands to see that both are godly. Discipline of both your lifestyle and your heart is necessary for spiritual growth!

BIBLICAL STUDY

Read 2 Timothy 2:21 carefully. Write the verse below in your own words. As you paraphrase this verse about the holy life, pray that God will give you a disciplined lifestyle.

PERSONAL APPLICATION

1. Ask yourself this thought-provoking question: "If I am the only Christ that many people will see, what kind of Christ do they see in me?" Your outward appearance should point others to Jesus. In what ways do you need to change your outward behavior?

2. With the help of the Holy Spirit, make a plan to engage in holiness in the following areas. Write down your plan and begin today.

   Bible Study:

   Prayer:

Witnessing:

Service:

3. What is your life's purpose? Formulate a one-sentence statement of the central focus of your life. All of your outward behaviors (priorities and planning) should revolve around this one purpose in life.

Dear Lord,

It is Your desire that my life be a reflection of Your love in the world around me. Give me the power to control my outward behavior so I will avoid unrighteousness, engage in holiness, and purpose for godliness all the days of my life.

Amen

CHAPTER 4

The Disciplined Heart
(Discipline of What? Inward Behaviors)

Above all else, guard your heart, for it is the wellspring of life (Proverbs 4:23).

Once there was a fat little girl named Rhonda. She grew up to be a fat big girl. All her life she struggled with her weight. She would diet and lose, then gain it all back. What a challenge!

One day, in her time with the Lord, that fat lady named Rhonda began to hear God convicting her of a lack of self-discipline. No self-control? All she needed was to lose a little weight. God clearly said, "You have a problem greater than your weight. You have a problem with your heart."

So, Rhonda confessed her weakness to God and began to claim His power for control in her life. God taught her a greater lesson than weight loss. He taught her the importance of self-control in all areas of life. With His supernatural power, Rhonda began to develop personal discipline.

As Rhonda learned about Spirit-controlled discipline, she lost weight. God gave her a new body and a new heart — a holy heart with godly inward thoughts and righteous outward behaviors. He created a new outward appearance and a new inward spirit. God continues to instill in Rhonda a desire for self-control through His infinite power and love. He continues to change her heart!

That was my story. Your story may be much the same but may involve another area of life. All too often we find our behaviors out of control. We work very hard to change these behaviors but it is our hearts God wants to change. Now it is time to examine the interior. We have considered our exterior — those outward behaviors that need to be disciplined. God's Word also instructs us to search our hearts because out of the heart comes evil thoughts and deeds (Matthew 15:19,20). The thoughts of our hearts as well as the actions of our bodies need control. *Many of us don't need a face-lift; we need a heart transplant!*

In New Orleans, we have many stately antebellum homes. Nothing is more disheartening than to admire a house from the outside only to be disappointed by the inside. Many homeowners spend a great deal of time and money repainting the exterior others see, while ignoring the needs of the interior where they live. A house will eventually crumble if no attention is given to the interior and its foundation. God would have us be beautiful inside and out. He admonishes us to clean our houses — to create pure hearts.

Did you learn about spring cleaning from your mother? My mother taught me that every house needs a spring cleaning. At least once each year every house should be cleaned thoroughly, inside and out. Clean the cabinets, wash the windows, dust the baseboards, shampoo the carpet. Do all the things often overlooked because of a busy schedule. During spring cleaning we uncover dirt that has accumulated during the year.

Let's do some spiritual spring cleaning! In this chapter, each of us will carefully examine her own heart to see what thoughts and feelings need to be controlled. Ask God to help you see with your eyes the desires of your heart. God wants to sharpen your sight — "Better is the sight of the eyes than the wandering of desire" (Ecclesiastes 6:9 RSV). Once you do this, God can help you control your passion for possessions, your feelings for your fellowman, and your concern for character.

Passion for Possessions

What are the passions of your heart? A passion is "an ardent love or affection; a strong affection or enthusiasm for an object, concept, or experience; any strongly felt emotion" (Collins dictionary, 1987). The passions of our hearts are usually physical desires manifest in material possessions, sexual exploitation, or financial obligation. These natural passions are temporal; they give only momentary pleasure.

Christians are commanded to purify their passions — to flee their flesh — to discipline their desires — to control their carnal natures. David acknowledged the importance of inward discipline when he wrote: "Let the words of my mouth, and the meditation of my heart, be acceptable in thy sight, O Lord, my strength, and my redeemer" (Psalm 19:14 KJV). Our outward behavior is known to others, but our hearts are known only to God. Our hearts must be approved by God. A godly heart requires discipline of our passions. Many times the passions of my heart are material things — extravagant clothes, fine jewelry, a beautiful house, an expensive car. Instead of longing to know God more fully, I long for material things. I often exchange treasure in the eternal for pleasure in the temporal. God has convicted me of my passion for possessions. He has offered me the power I need to redirect my passions toward Him.

For me, as for many women, one of the greatest temptations is clothes. I love beautiful clothes! I would rather do without almost anything else! I work hard to control my impulses while shopping. Though I have a specific clothing budget, it is sometimes insufficient to control my desire for clothes. Sometimes I must leave my purse, including my credit cards, at home when I got out shopping. Even though my actions may be controlled, I still have a heartfelt passion for these material possessions.

It is natural for us to desire things that we see and use. It is also natural for a boat without power to drift in the direction of the current or tide. A boat is usually designed with some sort of control so it can go where a person wants it to go, rather than going with the whim of the tide or wind. The boat of our lives is floating on an ocean with currents and tides, not on the still water of a pond. Doing what comes naturally will focus us on the physical and material. With God's supernatural power, we can concentrate on Christ. We can allow God to help us overcome our human tendencies and follow His plan for our lives.

In my struggle to gain control and lose weight, I realized that food had become my driving passion. I continually craved something to eat. There were times when the strongest desire of my heart was a hot fudge sundae or a chocolate truffle. I had allowed my physical passion to replace my passion for God. I could identify with Cathy in the cartoon strip when she went out in the snow to buy a candy bar, but decided that the weather was too severe to go out with a friend! I loved food!

My lack of inward control led to outward abuse. Because I loved food and thought about it constantly, I ate constantly. It was time for a change not only in what and how much I ate, but in what I thought about food. I prayed, "Lord, control the passions of my heart. Help me long for You, not for food." God changed my heart about food while He helped me control what I ate. If Christians will fill their hearts with God, there will be no need to fill their hearts with other things.

As Christians we must learn to control our passions! At times we are consciously aware of the affections of our hearts. It is easier to stand strong against evil when we recognize our enemy. But most often, we are unaware of our passions. If our hearts don't remain passionate for God, they will find satisfaction in other people and possessions. If we let down our guard of self-control, our hearts will be filled with ungodly desires and our thoughts may be translated into actions.

Gordon MacDonald wrote candidly about the deceit of the devil in his book, *Rebuilding Your Broken World*. He said, "There came a time when dragons, if you please, had come through my gates and had caught hold of my mind and my choice-making mechanisms" (page 89). Those ungodly passions often sneak in by night and catch us off guard. God's people must control their passions.

John Bunyan, author of *The Pilgrim's Progress*, once confessed that his sin was a natural result of his wicked heart:

> Sin and corruption would bubble up out of my heart as naturally as water bubbles up out of a fountain. I thought now that everyone had a better heart than I had. I could have changed hearts with anybody. I thought none but the devil himself could equalize me for inward wickedness and pollution of mind. I fell, therefore, at the sight of my own vileness, deeply into despair, for I concluded that this condition in which I was in could not stand with a life of grace. Sure, thought I, I am forsaken of God; sure I am given up to the devil and to a reprobate mind.

As did Bunyan, we must realize that we have sinful natures and evil hearts. Our inward wickedness is natural. But we are not forsaken by God. He gives us the power to control the wickedness of our hearts. God helps us overcome our sinful natures. Our responsibility is to "take heed," "set a watch," and "be vigilant" to discipline the passions of our hearts.

The desires of our hearts can quickly become a passion for possessions or a lust for love if we do not resist evil. In His Word, God warns us to "abstain from evil." He doesn't say "be careful" or "pray about it." He says, "Abstain!" That means run from evil! Don't touch it! Have nothing to do with it! We must use self-control to resist the temptation of the devil. Remember, the devil is like a roaring lion seeking whom he may devour (1 Peter 5:8).

God will help us have a disciplined heart; He will help us control our passions for possessions. He will also empower us to control our feelings for our fellowman and our concerns for our character.

Feelings for Fellowman

Many times God needs to control our thoughts and feelings about others. Our feelings toward our spouses, our children, our families, and our friends can become unkind and unloving. By nature, we are easily irritated by their actions, frustrated by their inadequacies, and hurt by their criticisms. It takes self-control to love people. God can help you exert self-control in your feelings for your fellowman.

When life becomes out-of-control, the first thought is to take out our frustrations on others. Blame, doubt, anger, pity, and jealousy are some of the ungodly feelings toward others that result from an uncontrolled heart. These unproductive feelings hurt others and hurt us. God can teach you to control these negative feelings and develop positive ones.

Early in my professional career I was working on the staff of a large children's hospital. While I loved my work with the children, I soon realized that the negative personalities of my colleagues were rubbing off on me. I found myself being critical, angry, and irritable because that was the atmosphere of my office. It is hard to resist the influence of others without conscious use of self-control. Once I became aware of my own weakness, I was better able to resist the negative influence until God moved me to a more positive environment.

The Holy Spirit wants to help you maintain self-control in your relationships. He can help you find something good in everyone, though you might have to look carefully. He can help you think loving thoughts about even the most unlovely people. God can help you forgive those who hurt you. Loving, forgiving, kind thoughts don't come easily. These godly feelings will develop through self-discipline.

There is good in everyone — though sometimes we must look very carefully and be truly determined to find it. One of my tasks in evaluating young children with handicaps is to diagnose the condition and make educational recommendations. A part of the process includes listing the child's strengths and weaknesses. Many times the severely impaired child seems overcome by weaknesses, but it doesn't take long to identify at least some strengths in even the most handicapped youngster. Often, the list of strengths outnumbers the child's obvious weaknesses. God would have us use self-control when we quickly recognize the faults of others, and, instead, He would have us find their potential.

There are many godly virtues Christians should express in their relationships with others. Scripture teaches us to love one another, to be kind to one another, and to serve one another. It takes self-control to show kindness in this unkind world.

In her book, *Don't Miss the Blessing*, JoAnn Leavell advises us to promote others as we (1) affirm them, (2) encourage them, and (3) minister to them. She says, "A proven way to help yourself is by helping other people, because when you seek happiness for others, you find if for yourself" (page 59). The discipline needed to promote others pays off in the end. You will be blessed as you bless those around you!

Loving feelings for your fellowman are an overflow of a heart committed to Jesus. As our hearts overflow with God's grace and glory, we feel love and mercy toward our fellowman. Christians desiring to mature spiritually must learn to control their feelings toward others. Eliminate the negative feelings and elevate the positive feelings. Remember that *your thoughts about others will reflect your thoughts about God*. The disciplined heart demands control of passions and feelings. The disciplined heart also demonstrates a concern for character.

Concern for Character

It has been said that "character is what a person is in the dark." In other words, who you are is best seen in what you do when you think no one is looking. Your true nature is exposed in private. Outward appearance is only a reflection of the inward person. It is true that the better you know someone, the more you know his character. You must learn to control your character.

God wants to help us control our characters — our temperaments — our personalities. Character is simply "the combination of traits and qualities distinguishing the individual nature of a person" (Collins dictionary). Our characters are made up of attributes and traits. Temperament is a synonym for character. Temperament can be defined as a person's character, disposition, and tendencies. It is the characteristic way an individual behaves. What is your character or temperament?

Are you moody or cheerful? Cautious or impulsive? Reflective or carefree? We have many different natures. Our differences make us interesting. But, no matter what our individual disposition, each of us has tendencies that need to be controlled. We must know our own temperament or character before we can control it. We must develop the positive traits and restrain the negative ones.

There are several basic types of temperaments. The four-temperament theory, which originated with Hippocrates before Christ was born, continues to be the most widely accepted explanation of human behavior. Tim LaHaye wrote about these basic personalities first in his book *Spirit-Controlled Temperament*, and later in a sequel, *Your Temperament: Discover Its Potential*. He described the four basic categories as sanguine, choleric, melancholy, and phlegmatic.

The *sanguine* is generally a warm, buoyant, lively, and happy person. The *choleric* is typically hot, quick, active, practical, strong-willed, self-sufficient, and very independent. The *melancholy* is an analytical, self-sacrificing, gifted, perfectionist type with a very sensitive emotional nature. And, the *phlegmatic* is the calm, easygoing, never-get-upset individual with such a high boiling point he almost never becomes angry. As you can imagine, there are many different combinations of these four basic temperaments.

Have you begun to identify your own personality type? Have you recognized the personalities of people you know? It is very important for Christians to understand their temperaments so their weaknesses can be controlled and their strengths can be captured.

Florence Littauer also discussed temperaments in her excellent book entitled *Personality Plus*. She summarized two reasons for studying about temperaments: "First, examine our own strengths and weaknesses, and learn how to accentuate our positives and eliminate our negatives; and, second, understand other people, and realize that just because someone is different does not make him wrong" (page 15). Christians must recognize the characteristics of their personalities which need to be controlled. As we learn about our temperaments, we can begin to exhibit the fruit of the Spirit in our lives, which includes self-control.

My nature is generally happy, positive, and outgoing. However, I have often found that my disposition changes when I lose control of my eating. Like many others, I become irritable, negative, and critical when I diet. I seem to have the attitude that if I am going to suffer by not eating, everyone should suffer. I am sure that everyone around me knows when I am dieting. They can tell it by my disposition. I must realize that my character or disposition is being affected more by my circumstances than by my Lord. As a Christian, I must consistently reflect the character of Christ, regardless of my circumstances.

The Bible says much about character. In Deuteronomy 10:12,13, Moses said, "And now, O Israel, what does the Lord your God ask of you but to fear the Lord your God, to walk in all his ways, to love him, to serve the Lord your God with all your heart and with all your soul, and to observe the Lord's commands and decrees that I am giving you today for your good?" It is clear that God wants us to be people who are committed to Him, who seek His guidance, who serve Him gladly, and who obey His teachings. He wants us to reflect His character.

Proverbs 10 gives instruction about character. It states that the wise person will "accept commands," is a "man of integrity" who "walks securely," one who will "store up knowledge," who "heeds discipline," and who "holds his tongue." While it is hard to walk in wisdom, store up knowledge, and obey instruction, self-control will help us develop this godly character.

Ruth was a woman of strong character. Because of her loyalty in marriage and her faith in God, she chose to return to Judah with her mother-in-law, Naomi. She was willing to leave her own birth family and homeland to care for Naomi even after her own husband died. God disciplined Ruth's heart. He gave her a righteous character. She was happy, helpful, unselfish, and kind regardless of her external situation. In the same way, God can control our characters.

Godly character was a trait my parents wanted me to develop. While my appearance and actions were recognized by them, my parents reminded me of the importance of my actual character. My father used an interesting illustration. He encouraged my sister and me to care for the package God had given us. Our life was described as a gift from God, a present we should carefully wrap. He explained that the appearance of the package was important. People like to open beautiful packages. But my father also cautioned us to take care of the inside — our hearts. God has brought that lesson to my mind often as a reminder of my responsibility to God for His precious gift to me. I must control my outward appearance, but I must also control my inward character.

God wants to control our characters — He wants to change our dispositions — He wants to increase the positive and decrease the negative traits in our temperaments. He can do it! He can help us control even the most difficult characteristics if we let Him.

Personally, I found that God could give me a disciplined heart. He helped me control my passion for possessions, my feelings for my fellowman, and my concern for my character. The Holy Spirit even took control of my passion for food. He changed my pattern of eating outwardly and my love for food inwardly. God does want to control our lifestyles and our hearts.

As God began to deal with me about my physical passions, my feelings for others, and my character, He made me back up from where I was to see where I had started. I realized that all the roads started in the same place — my heart. The best way to change where we are is to make changes where we start. When our hearts are truly right with God, a life that is right will follow. Proverbs 4:23 says, "Above all else, guard your heart, for it is the wellspring of life."

The condition of our hearts is of the utmost importance to God. Spiritual discipline is an outward reflection of an inward reality. The inner attitude of the heart is far more crucial than the mechanical movements of everyday life. It is critical that we as Christians allow God to control our inner attitudes even more than our outward behaviors. Through spiritual growth we receive God's gift of inner righteousness and godly character. Spiritual growth requires discipline and results in Christ-like actions and a godly heart.

Pray today that God will help you practice self-control in your heart — that He will discipline your passion for possessions, your feelings for fellowman, and your concern for character. Allow God to give you a heart transplant and not just a face-lift!

BIBLICAL STUDY

Thoroughly read Proverbs 10. As you read this chapter, list below the key words and phrases that describe the character of a disciplined believer.

Key Words   *Key Phrases*

PERSONAL APPLICATION

1. Carefully examine the passions of your heart. What do you most desire — earthly possessions or eternal life? Write your answer in the space provided below.

2. Do you have any negative feelings about others? Name one person whom you have wronged by your words or deeds. Think of

a positive response that God will help you employ. Write your response below.

3. What type of temperament do you have? Identify those negative traits that God can help you control. Record your answer here. Begin today to let God change your character.

Dear Lord,

"By the grace of God I am what I am" (1 Corinthians 15:10). Help me to accept myself as Your divine creation and to use Your unlimited power to control my passions, feelings, and character. Then I will be a vessel fit for Your service.

Amen

CHAPTER 5

Personal Willpower
(Discipline How? Step One)

For God did not give us a spirit of timidity, but a spirit of power, of love and of self-discipline (2 Timothy 1:7).

Many people have visions for their lives, but lack the will to do what they envision. They know what they want and believe it is possible. However, they skip over the disciplined steps leading to the ultimate goal, always trying to find an easy shortcut. Consequently, they never reach their full potential. *What a tragedy when high hopes are defeated by low efforts!* Self-discipline is essential to success in all areas of life.

Bookshelves today are filled with best-selling publications on "how to get rich quick." What we have learned is good advice only works if it is practiced. Of course, many of those books offer hopeless dreams, a futile pursuit of fame and fortune. Nevertheless, the reader can benefit from instructions about hard work and personal effort. In order for us Christians to succeed in life, we must exert some effort. We must use some of our God-given willpower.

If you were to ask me, "Why do people fail to accomplish their dreams?" I would respond, "They never take the first step — they don't use their own God-given power." Most of us quickly rationalize away our failures with explanations such as: "I just can't do it." "I don't have any willpower." "I don't have the strength to finish it." The time has come to give up those excuses and move on to a solution. God has given each of us enough willpower to succeed in His plan for our life. Believers are reminded of God's abundant power in 1 Thessalonians 5:24: "The one who calls you is faithful and he will do it." So you already possess all the power you need to be disciplined!

Willpower is defined as "the ability to control oneself and determine one's actions" (Collins dictionary). It can also refer to the *firmness* of will. I understand willpower to be the determination to "stick to" a task. Many people feel they have either weak willpower or no willpower. But, God has given all of His children an adequate supply of willpower. The extra blessing for believers is the additional gift of God's power.

People often think of the devil making Eve sin in the garden of Eden. But the devil didn't do it. Eve did. She chose sin over obedience to God. All Satan did was give her an opportunity to choose. Her lack of personal control brought sin into the world and cost humanity the beauty and security of the garden. Eve had the power available to flee from temptation. She could have used her own willpower so God could further empower her to be obedient.

During the time God was convicting me of my lack of self-control, I had a stimulating conversation with a colleague who had succeeded in losing a significant amount of weight. She related her experience to me: "I had lost control of my life. I began to release my frustration through eating. So I decided to do something about it. I decided to lose weight and get control of my life." My friend never realized the impact her statement would have on my life. I determined to use some self-control and I added to my willpower God's supernatural power to pursue discipline in my eating.

Self-discipline is the result of a conscious choice to do what ought to be done. Each person chooses to be controlled or uncontrolled in thinking and living. But the first step is a personal decision to be disciplined. In this chapter, let's analyze our own willpower. Prayerfully consider the personal commitment, the ideal conditions, and the lifestyle changes needed in your pursuit of self-control.

Personal Commitment

My personal understanding of the doctrine of man is that we have the freedom of choice. When God in His infinite wisdom created the world, He gave man the ability to govern his affairs through a series of choices. No other creation of God has this unique power. Man alone has been given the power of choice. It is God's divine plan for me to help determine the course of my life. Action is required on my part!

My Christian life involves more than waiting for God to move in my life. It also requires an active response to what God wants me to do. While He begins the action, I must respond to His initiative. I must accept God's grace gift of personal willpower and use it to gain control of my life.

There will always be excuses for our failures because we have an infinite ability to rationalize our shortcomings. The challenge is to move beyond those easy answers and search our hearts for the solutions to the problems. In most cases, we fail to achieve goals in our lives because we fail to do our part. When we do not use the willpower God has given us, success becomes impossible. We, in essence, choose to fail; we choose to disobey God.

Self-discipline, which results in spiritual maturity and personal growth, requires a sincere commitment. *Each individual must decide to be disciplined.* No one else can decide for you. That decision is the first step on the journey toward self-discipline. Once the personal commitment is made, God will give supernatural power to the believer. However, God cannot empower you if you don't take the first step. You must use the willpower the Creator has given you. Exercise your power of choice and choose to be disciplined!

We must make our own decisions. We have personal freedom and sole responsibility in decision-making. The Bible speaks about the two paths in life, the broad path and the narrow path. The broad path is the world's path of destruction leading to dissatisfaction in life and separation from God in eternity. The narrow path is the Lord's path of security leading to joy in life and presence with God in eternity. It is our responsibility and privilege to choose the path we will follow in life. While most people follow the world's path, Christians should follow the path of God, the less traveled path.

In his famous poem, "The Road Not Taken," Robert Frost concluded: "I took the road less traveled and that has made all the difference." Many factors influence the decision of which way to travel. But, the traveler ultimately must decide which road to follow. For the Christian, the disciplined, godly life is the road less traveled. Most people follow the undisciplined, ungodly life. If you choose to follow God's way to His heavenly kingdom, that will make all the difference.

In the Sermon on the Mount (Matthew 5-7), Jesus taught His followers about choices. He used parables to help distinguish the options: two ways, two trees, two professions, two builders. Individuals must choose one option. While God provides guidance and instruction, the believer actually makes the decision. Few choose the narrow gate — the disciplined, godly life. Many choose the wide gate which leads to destruction. God gives us the ability to choose, but He also gives us the knowledge to choose wisely.

Over the years, I mastered many excuses for losing control of my weight. You name it; I had used every excuse in the book. I believed that some people naturally had more willpower than others. However, I was incorrect in saying, "I have no willpower." I could not benefit from God's power in my life until I recognized the personal responsibility I had to accept. Once I admitted that I did have some responsibility and, therefore, the ability to control my eating, then God was able to add to my limited human powers, His divine supernatural power.

On October 12, 1987 (a Monday, of course), I took the initiative to begin the development of self-control in my life. The Lord had convicted me of my uncontrolled life, not just my uncontrolled eating. I prayed, "Lord, today I give You myself. I choose to use my willpower to give myself to You. And in Your power, Lord, teach me to be disciplined not only in my eating, but in my heart and my life."

Once I trusted God and took the first step, He helped me do the rest. I prayed in faith, believing that God would answer my prayer. The Bible promises us that God hears and answers our sincere requests. Psalm 37:4 became a promise I claimed: "Delight yourself in the Lord and he will give you the desires of your heart." He not only helped me lose weight, but He also gave me Spirit-controlled discipline in all areas of my life.

Marjorie Holmes has often encouraged me in my spiritual pilgrimage. In her book, *Secrets of Health, Energy, and Staying Young*, she relates a decision she made as a child. Mrs. Holmes shared her personal decision to stay fit. "All Dad's people were on the fat side; Mother's were lean. I decided to take after my mother's people. Deep in my soul I resolved never, never to be fat" (page 317). You may have seen Marjorie Holmes, a popular Christian speaker. She is trim and vivacious — the result of a decision she made in her childhood. Her success began with her personal commitment.

Spiritual or personal discipline is the result of a conscious choice

— a deliberate decision to act. A Christian will not grow in Christ without making that choice. Immature believers fail to rely on the willpower given to them by God. Their lack of personal commitment denies them the supernatural power of God. The decision to do the things of God is an act of the will.

Don't allow yourself to believe that your power alone is sufficient for a disciplined life! Human power is never adequate for the challenges of Christian living. Paul reminded us in 2 Corinthians 12 of our human weakness and God's divine strength. When he was facing a trauma he described as a "thorn in the flesh" (verse 7 KJV), Paul was assured by the Lord, "'My grace is sufficient for you, for my power is made perfect in weakness'" (verse 9). The apostle was able to accept and even boast about his weakness because God's power compensated for his inadequacy. We can exclaim with Paul, "When I am weak, then I am strong" (verse 10) because of the Spirit's power within us. This revelation should be a precious promise to all believers, not an easy excuse for poor discipline. Personal commitment is a prerequisite for self-discipline!

Before Paul could experience God's strength, he had to accept the reality of the thorn. Paul suffered from some weakness in his life that taught him humility and dependence (2 Corinthians 12:7). Years earlier on the Damascus road, Paul committed his life to following Jesus. When the "road less traveled" led to a time of suffering, the Lord provided the strength Paul needed to stay on his path. Because Paul was committed to following Jesus with blessings or thorns, he always found help for every circumstance he faced. Like Paul, we can commit to discipline even through suffering.

The first step towards self-discipline is a personal commitment — a deliberate decision to take action. You alone must take that step! Now that we have discussed the need for personal willpower, let's talk about the ideal conditions and the lifestyle changes necessary for disciplined Christian living.

Ideal Conditions

While God has given us personal willpower to which He will add His supernatural power, it is important to create an atmosphere that will encourage self-discipline. Jesus told us that "the spirit is willing, but the body is weak" (Matthew 26:41). He warned us to keep watching out for temptation (Mark 14:38). So as Christians, we must try to live in a way that minimizes our times of temptation or testing and maximizes our mastery of self-control. If we build an environment that encourages vigilance and restraint, we will find self-control easier to develop and maintain.

My husband loves football. He often quotes Vince Lombardi, legendary football coach of the Green Bay Packers, who once told his players, "Success breeds success." In football games and in daily lives, one accomplishment encourages another. The first pursuit of self-control prompts continued discipline. *Self-discipline breeds self-discipline.* Create an atmosphere in your life with ideal conditions which, in turn, promotes self-control.

A Christian must sometimes flee from temptation. We should avoid vulnerable situations in our daily lives. Often we must say good-bye to settings and people that tempt us (1 Timothy 6:11,12). For new believers, this may mean limiting contact with old friends who are a bad influence or abandoning places that foster immorality. It is crucial to eliminate optional temptations in order to control inevitable vulnerabilities. There are some circumstances in life you cannot bypass, but there are many situations you can avoid!

Gordon MacDonald relates a counseling experience in his book, *Rebuilding Your Broken World.* A guilt-ridden Christian man had become involved in a one-night affair while on a business trip. MacDonald encouraged the remorseful man to think back on how he could have avoided the temptation. "Examine that environment in which you made your choice and ask what could have been done to make your choice making different," challenged MacDonald (page 103). The man had, in fact, placed himself in a situation making it easy to make bad choices. If he had avoided the situation, he could have resisted the temptation.

One can make bad choices which result in sin. However, God would have us choose to avoid circumstances that tempt us to sin. Remember the prayer Jesus taught us — "'Lead us not into temptation'" (Matthew 6:13). You should turn from evil and turn toward good. Don't go places where sin abounds. Create an atmosphere of holiness that will encourage self-control. Then you will have done your part to maintain ideal conditions.

This same wise advice can apply to eating. A dieter, whose sincere desire is to change her eating habits, must alter routines and minimize contact with food. Take another path to avoid tempting foods. Leave a meeting when the refreshments are served. There is truth in that old adage, "Out of sight, out of mind." If we avoid temptation by altering our patterns, we can create more ideal conditions for the practice of self-control.

During college years, my service organization regularly sold donuts to raise money for worthwhile projects. Each member was given four dozen donuts to sell within a week's time. You can imagine what happened when all of us tried to sell our sweets to coeds in the same dormitory. It was an impossible task. As the deadline neared, we usually bought our own donuts and, of course, ate them ourselves. While this project was envisioned to benefit a worthy cause, it was disastrous for me!

At the time I had little self-discipline. I gained weight while raising money. I should have used some self-control in the situation. I could have avoided the temptation by contributing my money without consuming the food or suggesting a fund-raiser with a low-calorie product. The point is this: I could have and should have made an effort to avoid and even flee from the temptation. Self-control is easier when the conditions encourage us to do the right thing.

Another college experience comes to my mind. We had vending machines in the stairwell on each floor of the dormitory. The candy and chips became very appealing when studying for a test late at night or unwinding at the end of a long day of classes. There was a time during my junior year when I tried to control my eating. I remember how I purposely altered the route to my third floor room by walking up a different stairway to avoid those tempting machines. If you can't fight it, run from it! Avoidance helps your self-control.

Several guidelines may be helpful as you attempt to avoid situations which test your self-control and challenge your willpower.

1. *Identify your vulnerabilities.* Try to learn your own weaknesses. Once you know your weak points, you can begin to confront them.

2. *Avoid obvious temptations.* Do everything in your power to minimize your encounters with temptation. Many tempting circumstances can be successfully avoided if you take control.

3. *Pray about inevitable situations.* When you are unable to avoid a

person or setting that is tempting, seek God's power through prayer to protect you from the inevitable temptation.

4. *Confront problems as they occur.* Don't accept small compromises in your life that will distort your judgment. As sin in your life becomes apparent, seek God's forgiveness immediately and turn from your sin.

5. *Affirm your relationships with God and others daily.* Remind friends and family of your love regularly. Demonstrate your love in a variety of ways.

If you do not have an ideal environment for self-control, begin to build it yourself.

These five guidelines can help you flee from temptation and seek ideal conditions so you can be disciplined in your Christian life. As magnets repel each other and attract metal, so our lives should repel evil and attract righteousness. Decide now to commit yourself daily to a godly, disciplined life. Voice your commitment with King David who said, "As for me, I shall walk in my integrity" (Psalm 26:11 NAS).

Gardening is one of my favorite pastimes. I love for my window boxes to bloom and my flower beds to flourish. It is hard to provide the perfect conditions consistently for hearty growth — fertile soil, adequate rain, and proper sunlight. Professional gardeners often build hothouses to ensure ideal conditions for the plants. God calls His children to create a "hothouse effect" ensuring personal growth through disciplined living. Personal commitment, ideal conditions, and lifestyle changes are necessary for spiritual growth.

Lifestyle Changes

Believers who desire to grow in the likeness of Christ need to utilize their own willpower. Personal self-control can be developed through lifestyle changes. An integral part of the disciplined life is a godly lifestyle. A person's lifestyle is a witness in the world. You may need some self-control to change weaknesses in your lifestyle.

In the pursuit of a self-controlled life, a Christian must carefully consider her lifestyle. Specific steps should be taken to change ungodly attitudes, habits, and behaviors to godly feelings, practices, and actions through daily discipline. God expects His children to be "set apart" from the world, to lead righteous lives that reflect the Father's love in an unlovely world.

God's Word teaches us that, as followers of Christ, we must die to our old selves and live for our new selves. Paul told the church at Ephesus to leave their former lives and start new lives in Christ: "Put off your old self, which is being corrupted by its deceitful desires; . . . be made new in the attitude of your minds; and . . . put on the new self, created to be like God in true righteousness and holiness" (Ephesians 4:22-24). The old self is corrupt and evil; the new self is godly and righteous. It is essential to give our old life to God and replace it with a new lifestyle in Him.

For me, the ordinance of baptism is a beautiful picture of this transformation from the old life to the new life. As the believer is "buried in baptism" (immersed in the water), the old, sinful life dies. A new life begins when the believer is raised from the water — a new life in Christ. This symbol of obedience is an expression to the world of a changed lifestyle. One who submits to baptism commits to a different lifestyle.

Paul also instructed the Christians in Ephesus about their daily lifestyles. In Ephesians 4:1-3, he told them to "live a life worthy of the calling you have received." His description of a Christian lifestyle included humility, gentleness, patience, love, diligence, and peace. Are those the characteristics that describe your life? If not, exert your God-given willpower to begin the process of self-discipline.

Personal commitment to righteousness requires daily self-discipline, but we can become like Christ. In his book, *The Spirit of the Disciplines*, Dallas Willard tells us how to develop a godly lifestyle.

> My central claim is that we can become like Christ by doing one thing — by following him in the overall style of life he chose for himself. If we have faith in Christ, we must believe that he knew how to live. We can through faith and grace, become like Christ by practicing the types of activities he engaged in, by arranging our whole lives around the activities he himself practiced in order to remain constantly at home in the fellowship of His Father (page ix).

We must study the life of Christ as recorded in Scripture in order to duplicate His lifestyle. If you trust Jesus Christ with your life, then you must trust Him with your lifestyle!

The real issue you have to resolve is this: Do you believe that

John 10:10 is true? Jesus said, "'I came that they might have life, and might have it abundantly'" (NAS). If you believe this promise, then you will adopt Christ's lifestyle. God does not call us to a life we can't enjoy. His desire is for us to be satisfied and joyful. An obedient follower of Christ will seek to imitate His life, knowing that the results of disciplined living are abundant blessings.

Jesus' lifestyle was characterized by godly attitudes, disciplined habits, and unselfish behaviors. He led a simple life of sacrifice and service. He received strength from His Father in solitude and gave unselfishly of Himself to the masses. From Jesus we learn to be caring, consistent, and concerned. Is this a picture of your lifestyle? Does your life mirror the life of Christ? If not, you can become like Christ by deciding in your own heart to follow a Christ-like lifestyle.

An accomplished musician doesn't simply walk on the stage and perform. The great musician disciplines himself to practice constantly. In fact, the performer's lifestyle is affected more significantly by the time devoted to practice than by the actual applause arising from the performance. Sacrifice and commitment in one's daily life are required for excellence. Negative attitudes, bad habits, and harmful behaviors must be replaced by positive attitudes, healthy habits, and desirable behaviors. Without self-discipline, lifestyle changes cannot be made.

Many people have asked me how I have kept the pounds off. If I had to answer in one word, it would be "lifestyle." A lifestyle change was necessary for my weight to remain under control. I could lose the weight with minimum effort, but I couldn't keep it off unless I changed my lifestyle. I changed how I ate, what I ate, when I ate, and where I ate. You see, I changed everything about my eating habits. In this same way, a Christian must change her lifestyle in order to become more like Christ.

The secret to a godly life is a permanent lifestyle change. A disciplined Christian must live a holy life all the time in order to be like Christ and not like the world. A Christian must behave all the time as if Jesus were here in the flesh. We must always live like Christ and not like everybody else. We cannot be "on-call" for Christian living. Consistency is the key to a Christ- like lifestyle.

Romans 12:1,2 is a powerful passage about a godly lifestyle. Paul's direct statement to the Romans and to us today is clear — don't be conformed to the world, but be transformed by God:

> Therefore, I urge you, brothers, in view of God's mercy, to offer your bodies as living sacrifices, holy and pleasing to God — which is your spiritual worship. Do not conform any longer to the pattern of this world, but be transformed by the renewing of your mind. Then you will be able to test and approve what God's will is — his good, pleasing and perfect will.

As followers of Christ, our lifestyles must be drastically different from that of the world and consistently like the life of Christ. A godly lifestyle demands holy sacrifice.

Making these lifestyle changes is not easy. Some personal self-control and daily discipline is necessary. But, the best lesson comes from Christ Himself. The secret is to learn from Christ how to live our total lives and how to invest all our time and our energies of mind and body. Jesus was always prepared for His work. He was disciplined spiritually in personal prayer and Bible study. His lifestyle evidenced His love, care, and concern. Jesus was enabled to receive his Father's constant and effective support while doing His will. Jesus made the necessary changes to maintain a righteous lifestyle.

You need to know something about me — I am *not* a "morning person." My husband, Chuck, wakes up every morning with a smile on his face. I wake up slowly, with great effort, and with no evidence of a smile. In fact, Chuck says I don't even believe in God until ten o'clock in the morning! Each evening I try to go to bed early enough to get up the next morning on time. (I have to be up by 7:00 A.M. to get to work by 8:30 A.M.) I love to stay up late, but I need eight hours of sleep. What a dilemma! Every night I must use self-control to force myself to go to bed and every morning I must use self-discipline to get myself out of bed. While I don't have the power to adjust my body clock, I do have the power to change my lifestyle. If I change my lifestyle, then less self-control is needed to get up each morning.

Personal willingness to commit is the first step toward self-control. Sincere commitment, ideal conditions, and lifestyle changes are part of the process. I have learned in my spiritual pilgrimage that God can give us strength to pursue self-discipline. Paul's letter to Timothy affirmed this promise for me: "For God did not give us a spirit of timidity, but a spirit of power, of love and of self-discipline" (2 Timothy 1:7). The Lord adds to my finite willpower His infinite supernatural power so I can be disciplined. You, too, have the power to change your lifestyle. You have your power to commit, and you have His power to act on that commitment!

BIBLICAL STUDY

Read the following paraphrase of 2 Corinthians 12:9,10 and insert your name in the blanks. Claim these verses as divine promises for God's power to be disciplined:

God's grace is sufficient for me, for His power is perfected in weakness. Most gladly, therefore, _____ will rather boast about her weaknesses, that the power of Christ may dwell in her. Therefore, _____ is well content with weaknesses, with insults, with distresses, with persecutions, with difficulties, for Christ's sake; for when _____ is weak, then _____ is strong.

PERSONAL APPLICATION

1. Write a prayer of personal commitment. Promise God that you will use your own power to lead a disciplined, godly life.

2. List below at least three specific situations you now find yourself in that you know you should avoid. Begin today to flee those temptations.

3. How would you describe your lifestyle? Compare your lifestyle to the lifestyle of Christ. Answer yes or no to the following questions: Is your lifestyle characterized by humility? _____ gentleness? _____ patience? _____ love? _____ diligence? _____ peace? _____ Write a description of your present lifestyle. What can you do to improve it?

Dear Lord,

Thank You for giving me the power to control my life. Help me to make a personal commitment, to create ideal conditions, and to make lifestyle changes as I learn to be self-disciplined.

Amen

CHAPTER 6

Supernatural Godpower
(Discipline How? Step Two)

God is faithful; he will not let you be tempted beyond what you can bear. But when you are tempted, he will also provide a way out so that you can stand under it (1 Corinthians 10:13).

Several years ago my husband, Chuck, received a telephone call with a message that changed his life. The simple sentence, "Your father has had a heart attack," turned an ordinary day upside down. As Chuck drove the five hours to his hometown, uncertain of his father's condition, God demonstrated His supernatural power. Though Chuck's heart was heavy, God began renewing his spirit with the positive hope of Bible promises. The miles passed slowly, but the burden lifted quickly. These scriptures, learned in days past, became a present help:

Fear thou not; for I am with thee: be not dismayed; for I am thy God: I will strengthen thee; yea, I will help thee; yea, I will uphold thee with the right hand of my righteousness (Isaiah 41:10 KJV).

Humble yourselves therefore under the mighty hand of God, that he may exalt you in due time: casting all your care upon him; for he careth for you (1 Peter 5:6,7 KJV).

I can do all things through Christ which strengtheneth me (Philippians 4:13 KJV).

Chuck's early discipline in Scripture memory and meditation enabled God to help him in a time of need.

The Apostle Paul was very familiar with suffering and pain. Throughout his spiritual pilgrimage, he remained firm in his faith. His disciplined life resulted in personal growth and godly service. While he had an abundant life, he didn't have an easy life. He maintained confidence that his trials in life would never tarnish his faith in God. He believed what he wrote in the first letter to the Corinthians:

> No temptation has seized you except what is common to man. And God is faithful; he will not let you be tempted beyond what you can bear. But when you are tempted, he will also provide a way out so that you can stand up under it (1 Corinthians 10:13).

Paul learned that God's power was sufficient for all his needs.

God has chosen to share His supernatural power with you and me. It is our privilege to receive and experience His power. *God's divine power is the active force that makes self-control in our lives possible.* Personal willpower is not enough. We must also accept God's power in order to live abundant lives. The disciplined believer's challenge is to practice His presence, claim His power, and seek His joy.

His Presence

A baby immediately senses the presence of his mother, often before seeing her face or hearing her voice. That instant recognition is difficult to explain. I remember one occasion when I witnessed this behavior in our church nursery. A volunteer worker was trying her best to console a screaming infant. Suddenly the baby quieted. Relieved, the helper looked up and noticed the child's mother in the doorway. Without a word or a touch, the baby was comforted. The mother's physical presence calmed the crying child.

God comforts His children with His presence. While the Father is God ruling over us, and the Son is God acting for us, the Holy Spirit is God living within us. Jesus Himself taught His followers that God is present with the believer. God is omnipresent because He is everywhere (Psalm 139:7-12). Concerning the Holy Spirit, Jesus said:

> "And I will ask the Father, and he will give you another Counselor to be with you forever — the Spirit of truth. The world cannot accept him, because it neither sees him nor knows him. But you know him, for he lives with you and will be in you" (John 14:16,17).

The Holy Spirit is present permanently in the lives of all believers to advise, comfort, strengthen, and encourage.

The Holy Spirit indwells the individual at the time of salvation (Romans 8:9; 1 Corinthians 3:16). It is the Spirit of God Who reveals the Scripture to the believer and prepares the Christian for service. If you do not sense the presence of the Holy Spirit in your life, either you are not saved or you are not letting God's Spirit work. Have you accepted Jesus Christ as your personal Savior? Is His presence real in your life?

Jesus described His Spirit's presence in the life of the believer: "'Whoever believes in me, the Scripture has said, streams of living water will flow from within him'" (John 7:38). If the river of His Spirit is not flowing through you, then you may have "rocks in your river." You may have allowed sin to remain in your life, sin that is hindering the flow of the Spirit through you. An undisciplined life gradually dims your awareness of the presence of the Holy Spirit.

Have you ever been in a church service when the preacher was speaking, but your mind was a thousand miles away? Your ear registered the sound of his voice, and you would have noticed if he stopped talking, but you had no idea what he was saying. In the same way, the Spirit can be present in your soul trying to help you, but you can be unaware of what He is saying or doing. The Spirit is present, but you are missing the blessing of His presence.

In his sermon entitled "Rocks in the River," my husband teaches that Christians can remove obstacles so the Spirit can flow. His text, 1 John 1:9, says, "If we confess our sins, he is faithful and just and will forgive us our sins and purify us from all unrighteousness." Confession of sin and repentance in faith will remove the rocks from your river and allow God's Spirit to flow through you. When you ask God to forgive your sin and turn from your evil ways, then His Spirit's presence is known in your life.

God wants you to *experience* His presence. His presence is a present — a gift of grace. He wants you to pursue self-discipline as you practice His presence. In her book, *Don't Miss the Blessing*, JoAnn Leavell challenges her readers to "practice the presence of God and grow in faith through four spiritual disciplines: regular worship, silence, daily Bible reading, and prayer" (page 50). *God's presence promotes daily discipline, and discipline reveals His presence.* Don't miss the blessing of practicing the presence of God!

Though I know the Spirit is present with me at all times, there are certain times when I am especially aware of His presence. I often experience God's closeness at night when I am alone. Because my husband's preaching frequently takes him away from home, I have learned to depend on the Holy Spirit for strength. I can sing with conviction the words to a familiar hymn: "Just when I need Him most, Just when I need Him most; Jesus is near to comfort and cheer, Just when I need Him most." The presence of the Spirit often replaces my fear and loneliness. God's presence is real in the life of a believer.

Anne Ortlund in her personal notebook wrote of the Holy Spirit's work in her life:

> The light of God surrounds me;
> The love of God enfolds me;
> The power of God protects me;
> The presence of God watches over me;
> Wherever I am, God is.
> (*Disciplines of the Heart*, page 45)

Mrs. Ortlund also has experienced the power and presence of the Spirit. When God's Spirit fills the lives of believers, He enables them to practice daily self-discipline. Without His presence, self-control cannot be accomplished. God's presence promotes discipline!

As I changed my eating habits, I felt the presence of the Holy Spirit encouraging me and enabling me. Without His presence, I would have been alone and probably would have yielded to the temptation to overeat. Instead He walked with me as my Helper. There were times when I was so filled with the Spirit that I did not need to be filled with food. I remember numerous occasions when my feelings of hunger were replaced by the filling of His Spirit. As I was constantly refilled with the Spirit, I was able to gain control immediately and lose weight ultimately!

The reality of God's presence helps me as I pursue a disciplined life. I am not alone in my journey. The Holy Spirit is always with me. I must first exert my personal willpower, but then I can claim His supernatural power through the presence of the Holy Spirit. Remember, Christian, self-control is possible because His presence encourages you!

His Power

God's presence encourages me and His power strengthens me! If God is walking with you, then His Spirit can enable you. God is not only omnipresent, He is also omnipotent — all powerful. As Creator, He is in control of the whole world. As Father, He is sovereign over His children. As Helper, He provides power for all believers. For all power belongs to God (Psalm 62:11).

The power of God is real, though words cannot explain it. In *The Spirit of the Disciplines*, Dallas Willard tried to describe the supernatural power of God. Spiritual disciplines "enable us more and more to live in a power that is, strictly speaking, beyond us, deriving from the spiritual realm itself" (page 68). The power a Christian receives from God is more than human power, it is spiritual power. A Christian who yields her life to the Lord receives supernatural Godpower to maintain a disciplined life.

How can you possess Godpower? It is important to realize that spiritual power is not ours simply to use; it is God's gift to us for growth. He chooses to empower us so we can live a godly, disciplined life. You can receive His power as you commune with Him in prayer and claim His promises in Scripture. As you spend time with the Father, you experience the Godpower to be self-controlled. When a Christian is totally yielded to the Spirit, she is overshadowed by a force greater than herself.

One way to claim Godpower is through prayer. Prayer taps the power source of God. I once read this statement: "Apart from its religious significance, prayer is one of the most effective methods of tapping the wisdom and power that exists in the great reservoir of the unconscious." In prayer we receive God's supernatural power and release our own personal willpower. Don't underestimate the power of prayer! In fact, begin to utilize God's power through prayer.

What is prayer? Prayer is not a one-way conversation of requests to God. It is not a dialogue of disappointments in life. Instead prayer is a two-way conversation between the Father and His child. Prayer is bringing the concerns of our heart and soul before the Lord Who loves us and wants to help us. Many believers fail to understand the true meaning of prayer. Self-discipline is necessary to experience the power of prayer.

Prayer draws us away from the strong emotional pull of temptation and pulls us toward the unlimited power source of God. Through the power of prayer we are able to channel our drives to God's ultimate purpose. Communication with God takes time. Time with God must be scheduled regularly. Make time to pray! Prayer works; yet it is virtually an untapped resource of God's power for disciplined living.

Personally I can say, there is power in prayer! I have felt the power of prayer. As I tried to gain control of my eating, I developed my prayer life. I prayed often and continually that God would replace my hunger for food with a desire for Him. Each morning I prayed for Godpower to be self-disciplined during the day. As I faced any temptation, I prayed for immediate strength. I remember several times when my prayers seemed somewhat silly. I prayed for steamed broccoli to taste like potatoes au gratin, and for fresh fruit to satisfy like chocolate cake. God empowered me through prayer to learn self-discipline. Prayer drew me away from temptation and closer to God!

If there is such Godpower in prayer, why don't Christians pray? John Stott, an outstanding British preacher, answered that question in a sermon preached at All Souls Church in London. He spoke of the great paradox of prayer. A part of us wants to pray because of the joy in praying. But a part of us doesn't want to pray because of the conviction in praying. Satan chooses to distract Christians from prayer rather than tempt them to evil. We must win the "battle of the threshold" — opening our door to God — in order to receive His power through prayer.

Stott clarified this "battle of the threshold" with an illustration. Imagine that God is within a walled garden. The devil stands in the only doorway, trying to stop you from entering before God. Each time you enter the presence of God through prayer, you must pass through the gate guarded by Satan. Only when you win the battle of the threshold can you get through to God and receive the power of His Spirit. The good news is that Satan's opposition is only a bluff! Every believer is guaranteed access to the Father through Jesus Christ (Ephesians 2:18). All we have to do is push on through Satan's distractions.

Often my prayer time is interrupted with Satan's distractions. Sometimes I am disturbed by the telephone ringing or the sound of the doorbell. However, most of the time Satan distracts me from within my heart. I begin to think of other things — chores to do, calls to make, places to go. When I allow Satan to distract me from my communion with God, then he has won the battle of the threshold. Fortunately, God has given me the power to ignore Satan's distractions and win the battle of the threshold. During my time with God, I receive His strength. Isaiah 26:3 becomes a promise I want to claim: "You will keep in perfect peace him whose mind is stead-fast, because he trusts in you."

God's promises are another source of His power. The Bible is filled with precious promises of God. Scripture says, "Through these he has given us his very great and precious promises, so that through them you may participate in the divine nature and escape the corruption in the world caused by evil desires" (2 Peter 1:4). As you claim God's promises, you receive His power to overcome temptation.

You may want to memorize several Bible promises to release His power in any time of need. God's Word often empowers me in moments of weakness. There is power in His promises. I have selected only a few from the thousands of promises written in the Bible. Choose one or two verses to memorize. You may want to write them on a card and keep the Scripture visible. Then call it to mind when you need it most.

> Psalm 28:7: The Lord is my strength and my shield; my heart trusts in him, and I am helped.

> Psalm 145:18: The Lord is near to all who call on him, to all who call on him in truth.

> Matthew 6:13: Lead us not into temptation, but deliver us from evil: For thine is the kingdom, and the power, and the glory, for ever (KJV).

> James 4:8: Come near to God and he will come near to you.

> Hebrews 4:16: Let us then approach the throne of grace with confidence, so that we may receive mercy and find grace to help us in our time of need.

> 2 Timothy 1:7: For God did not give us a spirit of timidity, but a spirit of power, of love and of self-discipline.

God's precious promises empower us to maintain discipline!

The encouragement of family and friends is so important to me. On many occasions, I have been strengthened by the affirmation of those I love. Not long ago, I faced a difficult decision at work. I shared my crisis with a special friend. One morning as I was getting dressed, she called to pray with me and strengthen me in my time of need. Her words encouraged me greatly. If the encouraging words of a friend mean so much, how much more will God's Word help us! It cannot fail! As God said to Isaiah the prophet:

As the rain and the snow come down from heaven, and do not return to it without watering the earth and making it bud and flourish, so that it yields seed for the sower and bread for the eater, so is my word that goes out from my mouth; it will not return to me empty, but will accomplish what I desire and achieve the purpose for which I sent it (Isaiah 55:10, 11).

Even during suffering and temptation, God's power is available through your fervent prayers and His faithful promises. You can win any battles and conquer all hardships if you seek His power through prayer and His strength through promises. Self-control is possible by the power of the Holy Spirit! The believer can claim the promise of God's presence and lay hold upon the power to pursue discipline.

His Joy

Thomas Aquinas wrote this very intriguing statement in his book, *The Wisdom of the Saints*: "No one can live without delight and that is why a man deprived of spiritual joy goes over to carnal pleasures." God created us with a desire for happiness. He wants us to know joy and pleasure, but not apart from Him. A Christian who is not experiencing the "joy of his salvation" will seek pleasure in other ways. Through self-discipline, we can have the joy of the Lord.

The young husband of Princess Caroline of Monaco was killed in a powerboat race in France. His untimely death was a tragic loss for his wife and for their three children, all under six years of age. Several months before his death, Stefano Casiraghi was asked about his dangerous pastime. He responded that he was aware of the risk but loved the challenge. He told the reporter, "I am traveling at speeds of 110 miles per hour and more. It is much too fast and I realize it is getting much too dangerous. I am afraid, many times I am afraid, but it is my passion." That young man with wealth and power risked his life for a few moments of pleasure. More tragically, he had announced this race was to be his last . . . and it was. Unfortunately, he chose to experience one more thrill before retiring as a world champion powerboat racer. People are driven by their passions for joy.

I love to laugh! I enjoy happy occasions and fun friends. Joy invigorates me! But it is very difficult to simulate joy in an unpleasant situation. Have you ever been in a situation where you had to pretend to be happy? Nothing is more difficult than to try to act like you're having fun when inside you're miserable. I remember one occasion when I had to rejoice with a friend over her promotion when I was facing great frustration in my own work. It is hard to act happy when you're hurting, even though you want to be joyful.

God knows that joy is important to us. In fact, He wants to give us abundant, lasting joy. As Christians, we are to seek His joy, not our own pleasures. We are to claim His eternal blessings, not our temporary thrills. *You will find self-control obtainable if you seek spiritual joy!*

You may ask, "What is spiritual joy?" I believe spiritual joy is the complete satisfaction that comes from knowing that God has everything in control. It is a deep feeling of happiness regardless of the circumstances. Joy is not the result of confidence in my control. It is confidence in God, for He controls everything! If He controls everything, then somehow, some way, He will work things out for me. Paul said it best in Romans 8:28: "And we know that all things work together for good to them that love God, to them who are the called according to his purpose" (KJV).

Like self-control, joy is part of the fruit of the Holy Spirit (Galatians 5:22,23). Joy, then, is a blessing from God, an evidence of His work in us. Spiritual joy gives strength. As Nehemiah the prophet said, "The joy of the Lord is your strength" (Nehemiah 8:10).

Spiritual joy should be natural for a believer who is filled with the Holy Spirit. Augustine of Hippo, a fourth-century theologian, said, "The Christian should be an alleluia from head to foot!" Because of God's presence and power in our lives, we can be overflowing with joy. The joyous Christian life is a real witness of His grace in this unhappy, carnal world.

How do you seek spiritual joy? While joy is a reason for self-control, it is also a result of self-discipline. Spiritual joy is both a motivation for daily discipline and a reward of self-control. In the spiritual life, only one thing will produce true joy, and that is obedience. As a believer follows Christ, she receives spiritual joy. Your desire for joy should motivate you to be disciplined.

Hannah Whitall Smith wrote an inspiring book about spiritual joy entitled *The Christian's Secret of a Happy Life*. Though written in 1870, her message continues to encourage believers to seek spiritual joy through daily discipline. "Joy comes through obedience to Christ and joy results from obedience to Christ. Without obedience, joy is hollow and artificial" (page 136). Happiness without spiritual joy is unsatisfying and temporal. True spiritual joy is satisfying and eternal. Seek *spiritual* joy!

A warning must be sounded to those who would seek spiritual joy without seeking the Father. While spiritual joy is a fruit of the disciplined life, it should not be our goal. Just as Paul said in Philippians: "I press on toward the goal to win the prize for which God has called me heavenward in Christ Jesus" (3:14). The goal is knowing God; the prize is spiritual joy. You don't receive the prize until you have reached the goal!

Chuck and I knew a young woman at Baylor University who went to college so she could get married. She didn't go to school for an education; she went to find a husband! (You may have known other women with a similar motivation.) How sad that her goal was the prize! If she had focused on and worked toward the goal of her education, she may have found a husband. But as far as we know, she has never married. When Christians focus their eyes on God, He gives them spiritual joy.

Spiritual joy cannot be received until you are spiritually prepared. Through the disciplines of prayer, Bible study, service, and witnessing, a Christian prepares her life to receive God's joy. An undisciplined believer cannot experience spiritual joy.

A personal experience illustrated for me the need for preparation. While I was staying at a cottage in the countryside of England, the gardener came by to plant bulbs. She was unable to plant the flower bulbs because the soil was too hard. The ground was too dry for the bulbs to grow. Just as soil must be prepared for planting flowers, the soul must be prepared through spiritual discipline for receiving joy. How many times has God come by to plant a spring bulb in your soul, but turned away because your soul was too dry?

A Christian has many resources for learning self-control. Personal willpower is a limited, natural source of strength for every believer. But *supernatural Godpower is an unlimited, eternal source of strength for disciplined believers.* When you depend on Godpower, His presence will encourage you, His power will strengthen you, and His joy will sustain you. Now that should make you want to live a disciplined life!

BIBLICAL STUDY

Carefully read 1 Corinthians 10:13 and then answer the following questions:

1. Who provides the power?

2. Who receives the power?

3. How does He give the power?

4. Why does He give the power?

PERSONAL APPLICATION

1. Recall a time when you were keenly aware of God's presence in your life. In the space below, write your account of this experience as you thank the Lord for His presence.

2. Choose one of the following scriptures that confirm God's power and presence. Write a paraphrase of the verse below. Memorize the verse and prepare to experience Godpower.

Psalm 28:7   Psalm 62:11   Psalm 145:18

3. Write your own definition of "spiritual joy." Begin today to experience God's joy through your practice of self-discipline.

Dear Lord,

I am ready to use my personal willpower, but I also need Your supernatural Godpower. I claim Your presence to encourage, Your power to strengthen, and Your joy to sustain.

Amen

CHAPTER 7

People's Persuasive Power
(Discipline How? Step Three)

> Therefore encourage one another and build each other up, just as in fact you are doing (1 Thessalonians 5:11).

People are greatly influenced by each other. One look at teenagers and you will be convinced of the persuasive power of people. Because teenagers want desperately to be accepted, they are easily led by their peers. It is not enough to wear blue jeans to school. They must wear the same brand of blue jeans as their friends. Young people usually follow the leadership of others, right or wrong.

As adults, we can be more affected by our friends than we realize. Common interests or values usually form the basis of friendship. Once a friendship is formed, we will do whatever we can to maintain the relationship and commonality. The "keep up with the Joneses syndrome" is an adult version of the teenage "look alike, act alike, sound alike syndrome." Because of the natural persuasive power of people, it is important to surround ourselves with godly friends and Christian models.

Most of us have at least one person we admire and hope to model. As Christians, we can find godly examples in the Bible. We can also look around the church fellowship for individuals with Christ-like characters. These people should be our role models. They can be the counselors from whom we seek advice. These godly individuals are the people we allow to have persuasive power over us. A Christian should imitate Christ but earthly models are helpful, too! We need godly heroes and heroines.

Whom do you admire? Whom do you try to imitate? I can think of several Christian friends who have been important Christian

93

role models in my life. As a teenager, I remember a beautiful young woman in our church who was a positive influence upon me. Beth was not only lovely in appearance, but she was also poised, bright, happy, and godly. I respected her and aspired to be like her. In college I had two friends who were good examples. They were active, studious, fun-loving, and considerate. Now I have several peers whom I admire and respect. Their Christ-like characters and loving spirits are a great influence on me. All of these individuals have one trait in common — they are all dedicated Christian women. Our heroines should be first and foremost committed to Christ. Then their persuasive powers will be God-directed.

How many times each day do you look in a mirror? Even though you may want to avoid your image, you undoubtedly look in a mirror throughout the day — while getting dressed in the morning, after your walk, before going out, and while driving to the store. We look in mirrors to compare how we want to look with how we actually do look. The periodic "reality check" lets us make the appropriate adjustments necessary to maintain the appearance we desire. Our closest friends should be mirrors reminding us of what we want to be and helping us become more of what God wants us to be.

Do you ever dramatically change your hairstyle? You return from the hairstylist and hardly recognize yourself in the mirror. In fact it may take days to adjust to your new appearance. I've had this experience many times. My husband says my hairstyle changes as often as the weather in New Orleans! I have caught a quick glimpse of the new me in a mirror and been surprised. God wants to surprise us by making of us someone we never imagined. He can do that as we discipline ourselves to follow Him, and as we imitate godly people we know.

In the journey toward self-control, personal willpower and supernatural Godpower are essential. However we also benefit from the persuasive power of people. Godly friends can nurture and empathize as well as monitor and praise. The encouragement of others can provide strength and accountability. Without others, life has less meaning. We would probably be unable to survive the demands of our hectic lives without the support of other people. We must depend on others for acceptance, affirmation, and accountability. There is strength in numbers. People can help you learn self-discipline.

Acceptance

One of the most important qualities in a friend is acceptance. Everyone needs someone who really understands her feelings and needs. Unconditional love and acceptance make the risk of change and the painfulness of growth possible. A true friend "loves at all times" (Proverbs 17:17). When love is not dependent on selfish desires, love can truly build up. As you seek to learn self-discipline, it is extremely helpful to have a friend who accepts you and understands your quest.

Ski instructors are the most accepting, affirming people I have ever met. Chuck and I snow ski every year, and we have both noticed that ski instructors are patient and kind no matter how poorly a student may ski. They never criticize a weakness; they simply find a strength. They can teach even the most uncoordinated person to ski. What we all need in life is a "ski instructor" — someone to accept us unconditionally!

When I began my search for self-discipline several years ago, I started to diet with a friend. For my friend, we were just on a diet. She wanted to lose weight. She didn't understand that my motivation and heart's desire was to gain self-control. It is not surprising that she didn't stick with her diet. At first she encouraged me as I lost weight; we celebrated together when we lost pounds. But soon she became discouraged. When she didn't lose weight, she felt she had failed. She was unable to continue encouraging me because she didn't understand my purpose. True empathy and understanding are essential to lasting friendship. *Sincere love and acceptance give people the power to persuade.*

Romans 12:15 says, "Rejoice with those who rejoice; mourn with those who mourn." In this verse Paul expressed a basic characteristic of friendship — empathy. As Christians we are challenged to develop our understanding of others so we can help them. You can better strive toward self-control when those you love understand you. Unconditional acceptance and love are great strengths in a world which fails to understand unselfish motivation.

One of my dearest friends is so special because she always understands me. While we are different in many ways, she seems to know my needs and recognize my desires. She shares my joys and my sorrows. At this time, our lifestyles are worlds apart. She is at home raising her three children while I am at work in the professional world or traveling in ministry. She understands my activities and supports me in them. Before a recent trip, she gave me a beautiful book to read as I relaxed on my vacation. What an unselfish gesture! I'm sure that she would have loved to get away herself and relax with that book! Yet she never seems jealous or frustrated by my "freedom." Instead she accepts my lifestyle and understands my needs. Her acceptance is such a blessing to me!

A spirit of acceptance allows you to share from your heart and soul. When you are confident that a friend understands, you can discuss even the most personal concerns without fear that she will judge you wrongly. It is helpful as you learn to be self-disciplined to find someone who understands you — someone who has a similar desire for spiritual maturity. Acceptance and understanding from that special friend will strengthen you in your pilgrimage.

Though my friend Sandra has never been overweight in her life, she understood my need to be controlled in my eating. She encouraged me and helped me along the way. She chose to eat a salad with me rather than to eat Mexican food with another friend. She passed on dessert with me and often cooked healthy meals for me. Her understanding of my commitment to self-control encouraged me to stay on track. The understanding of friends can strengthen your self-discipline. Friends can be a positive or negative influence on your life. If they understand your purpose, they will encourage you along the way.

On the other hand, God would have you use your self-control to accept others. It is impossible to minister to others in Jesus' name if you don't love and accept them. How sensitive are you to the needs of those around you? Are you aware of the burdens of family or friends? Do you accept all other people as children of God, loved by Him, and needing your care? Be obedient to your Father as you love and accept all His children. Christians should try to follow the Golden Rule: "Do unto others as you would have them do unto you." Accept others as you would have them accept you.

Christ taught us to accept others as His special creations. In His life, Christ demonstrated true acceptance of sinners as well as saints. When He met the woman at the well, Jesus ministered to her as He would have to any other person (John 4:7-30). His gesture was controversial in His day. According to social practices, He should have ignored her. A man did not speak to a woman in public. According to cultural differences, He should have avoided her. He was a Jew, while she was a Samaritan. According to moral standards, He should have condemned her. He was the sinless Son of God, while she was an adulterous woman. Instead Jesus recognized her, loved her, and helped her. He demonstrated that *the affirmation of others is always appropriate*. Even amidst an unaccepting culture, Jesus showed unconditional love to everyone He met.

One of the young girls with whom I work at church illustrated true acceptance. She tried to explain about a handicapped child to a visitor. In her own simple way, she expressed an attitude of unconditional love when she said, "Melanie is our special friend. She's mentally retarded, but she's really very smart." Each of us should have the same sincere acceptance so we can minister in Christ's name. Acceptance by others and unconditional love for others are essential ingredients in self-control. The affirmation of others also provides motivation for personal discipline.

Affirmation

Affirmation is a natural result of acceptance. When you accept individuals unconditionally, you are able to affirm and encourage them. Spiritual maturity is promoted by the encouragement of others. Affirmation is a ministry to the soul. In the same way that God affirms us for who we are, so we are to affirm others in love.

Exhortation or encouragement is a spiritual gift. Many Christians have the special ability to encourage others. Aren't we glad? I am grateful for the precious people who have been an encouragement to me. I am constantly affirmed by the ladies in our weekly Bible study. I benefit from the kind compliments of the student wives I teach. As a teacher, receiving their words of appreciation and notes of gratitude, as well as observing their faithful attendance, rewards my effort and motivates my study. I find that I discipline my time for Bible study as a result of their affirmation. The encouragement of others is another means of learning self-control.

The Bible records many people who were encouragers. Barnabas, whose name literally means "son of encouragement," is an inspiring example of encouragement. In Acts 11:22-30, we read of the many ways Barnabas encouraged the Christians in Antioch. He shared their joys, promoted their faithfulness, and confirmed their ministries. Are you considered by others to be an encourager? A part of your spiritual discipline should include affirmation of other people.

In 1 Thessalonians 5:11, Paul told believers to "encourage one another and build each other up." Affirmation is important to the fellowship of believers. Paul also told Christians to encourage their leaders:

> Now we ask you, brothers, to respect those who work hard among you, who are over you in the Lord and who admonish you. Hold them in the highest regard in love because of their work. Live in peace with each other. And we urge you, brothers, warn those who are idle, encourage the timid, help the weak, be patient with everyone. Make sure that nobody pays back wrong for wrong, but always try to be kind to each other and to everyone else (1 Thessalonians 5:12-15).

Christ-like behavior includes appreciation and affirmation of others in love. Encouragement strengthens the weak and is appreciated by all.

Hebrews 10:23-25 is another powerful passage about affirmation. A believer is to have a sincere heart and an encouraging spirit:

> Let us hold fast the confession of our hope without wavering, for He who promised is faithful; and let us consider how to stimulate one another to love and good deeds, not forsaking our own assembling together, as is the habit of some, but encouraging one another; and all the more, as you see the day drawing near (NAS).

We must persist in our affirmation of others. Believers can encourage each other in ministry and service. As we encourage others, we strengthen the fellowship of believers and build the body of Christ.

My husband, Chuck, is a great encourager to me. He affirms my person and my purpose daily. While I was learning self-control, he gave me support and confidence. However, he had to adjust many of the ways in which he shows his love. Before I began to control my eating, Chuck often left food gifts for me — a box of candy, a carton of ice cream, or a bag of cookies. He has changed his love gifts to cards, magazines, and notes. As I was losing weight, he helped me celebrate by buying new clothes for me — after fifteen pounds, a jumpsuit; after twenty-five pounds, a pair of slacks; then, after thirty-five pounds, a new suit. His gestures of love were a tremendous encouragement as I was practicing self-control.

The affirmation of others helps you develop self-control as you mature spiritually. You could do it alone, but God wants you to do it with His supernatural power and the encouragement of others. Chuck often says, "For every Lone Ranger, God provides a Tonto." God doesn't want us to live life on our own. He wants us to have fellowship with each other. In Hebrews 3:13 we are told to "encourage one another daily." Without unconditional acceptance and regular encouragement, we cannot serve or be served.

Accountability

Friends offer acceptance and affirmation, but they also ensure accountability. Do you have any idea why support groups are so popular? They provide acceptance and affirmation plus accountability. Group participation holds the member responsible for action. Groups like Weight Watchers and Alcoholics Anonymous provide accountability to individuals who want to lose weight or stop drinking. Without outside monitoring, self-control is more difficult. If you must weigh-in weekly or report progress regularly, you will be more motivated to remain controlled. *Accountability to others reminds us of our responsibility to God.*

In their book, *Love Hunger*, Drs. Minirth, Meier, Hemfelt, and Sneed discuss the necessity of support groups for individuals recovering from food addiction. Once people begin to control their behavior, outside encouragement is extremely helpful. Everyone benefits from the empathy of others.

> Even a person who is in a very loving family relationship will need the fellowship of walkers who have been over the same paths they have been. People in your family are in one sense too close to your problem because of living with you and in another sense, too removed from it because they haven't experienced the same addiction (pages 172,173).

Personally I need to be held accountable for my behavior. I am much more disciplined in my Bible study when I must teach a class or discuss my homework. On several occasions, I have joined with a partner in a weekly Bible study. I will always complete my assignment if I must show it to a friend. There have been times when I stayed up late to complete an assignment so I would not disappoint a friend. I am more faithful in exercise if I attend aerobics with a friend. Only an extreme circumstance will cause my absence. Accountability promotes self-discipline.

The Bible reminds the Christian of her accountability to God. Paul wrote in Romans 14:12, "So then, each of us will give an account of himself to God." In the gospel of Matthew, the disciple recorded these words of Jesus: "'I tell you that men will have to give account on the day of judgment for every careless word they have spoken'" (Matthew 12:36). It is clear that God keeps up with every word spoken and every deed done. If God is your divine accountant, recording your debits and credits, your sins and merits, how does your ledger entry look? Remember, you are accountable to God for all your actions.

Thank the Lord! As believers, we have been forgiven of our sins because of Christ's death for us on the cross. He died in our place, paying the penalty for our sins. Through His forgiveness, our accounts have been "paid in full." While the Christian is no longer under the guilt of sin, she is not given a license for ungodly living. Our lives should evidence the saving power of Jesus. We should be godly and obedient as an expression of love to a Savior Who died for us. Our lives should reflect God's love to others.

In the same way that God's judgment holds us accountable, so the approval of others holds us accountable. As a child, you were accountable to your parents for your behavior. As a citizen, you are accountable to the officials of government for your actions. As a student, you are accountable to the teacher for your knowledge. As a wife, you are accountable to your husband for your love. In life, you are held responsible for your relationships.

One reason I am hesitant about sharing my personal pilgrimage in self-control is because by doing so I become more accountable for my commitment. The more I share what God has taught me, the more other people hold me responsible. But the accountability is helpful to my continued self-discipline. I remember two humorous examples of my accountability to others. You may have similar memories.

At Christmas time when I began my controlled eating, I decided to eat one of Mrs. Kelley's traditional teacake cookies. I carefully planned when and where I would eat my one cookie of the Christmas season. So on Christmas day, I made a cup of hot apple cider and selected a perfect cookie, shaped like an angel with red icing on it. Just as I took my first bite, a brother-in-law walked by and commented, "You're gonna gain it all back." Then a niece asked, "Are you really eating a cookie?" After all my anticipation, I didn't even enjoy my one Christmas cookie. My family held me accountable for what I ate.

Last year I led a seminar on self-control for women. Of course, I talked about the importance of accountability. That night I took a few friends to the Morning Call Cafe for coffee and beignets (New Orleans French-style donuts). As I was passing out the beignets, several ladies from the seminar walked up to me, pointing fingers of accountability. I hadn't even eaten a donut, but they held me accountable for my incriminating behavior. What an embarrassment to the teacher! We must practice what we preach.

God expects His children to act like His children. Our behavior is a reflection on Him. In the same way that your parents may have taught you to uphold your family name, so God wants you to preserve His image. You are responsible for your actions. He will judge you and others will admonish you; so be on guard. Your accountability to others can help you remain disciplined. Allow their affirmation to motivate your actions. While your own willpower is necessary and supernatural Godpower is available, the persuasive power of others is essential to the practice of self-discipline.

BIBLICAL STUDY

Read the following scriptures about affirmation and encouragement. What do these verses teach you about being an encourager?

a. Acts 14:22

b. 1 Thessalonians 4:13-18

c. 1 Timothy 4:13

d. Hebrews 10:24,25

e. Hebrews 12:12-15

PERSONAL APPLICATION

1. Do you have trouble accepting others? Think of at least one person you find difficult to love. Ask yourself why you are unable to show acceptance to this individual. Record your responses below then seek God's help in showing unconditional love.

2. Read Acts 11:22-30 and answer this question: How did Barnabas encourage the Christians in Antioch? Now record your answer below, then write your own definition of the word "exhortation" based on your Scripture study.

3. To whom are you accountable for your behavior? Other than God, there are people in your life who hold you accountable. Who are they and how does their knowledge of you and your actions

promote your self-control? Write their names below as you thank God for their encouragement and your accountability.

Dear Lord,

Thank You for persuasive people power. Help me to realize that their acceptance and affirmation can be tools to teach me self-discipline. And use me to encourage others.

Amen

CHAPTER 8

Personalized Discipline
(Discipline of Myself)

Then he said to them all, "If anyone would come after me, he must deny himself and take up his cross daily and follow me" (Luke 9:23).

In a straightforward statement, Jesus Christ told His followers how to personalize discipline. He instructed them to make a deliberate choice to deny themselves and follow Him. Their choice required both sacrifice and commitment. Though Matthew and Luke recorded His words somewhat differently, both wrote the message clearly. The choice to follow Christ is a choice with consequences:

"And anyone who does not take his cross and follow me is not worthy of me. Whoever finds his life will lose it, and whoever loses his life for my sake will find it. He who receives you receives me, and he who receives me receives the one who sent me" (Matthew 10:38-40).

Then he said to them all, "If anyone would come after me, he must deny himself and take up his cross daily and follow me. For whoever wants to save his life will lose it, but whoever loses his life for me will save it. What good is it for a man to gain the whole world, and yet lose or forfeit his very self?" (Luke 9:23-25).

Christ demands a definite decision. If you choose to accept Him, you sacrifice yourself and follow Him faithfully. If you cannot make the commitment, then don't choose to follow Christ.

Life is filled with many choices. Some decisions have major, long-term, eternal impact. Other decisions have minor, short-term, temporal results. One thing is certain, while we may benefit from wise counsel, each of us is ultimately responsible for making our own decision. Many decisions require sacrifice. All decisions demand commitment.

The most life-changing choice made by a Christian is the decision to accept Jesus as Savior. The salvation experience begins with recognition of need and involves repentance from sin. By repentance the Bible means turning away from life on our own terms to live according to God's terms. He becomes our Lord and Master — our "boss." This personal choice includes sacrifice of the old life and commitment to a new life.

A convert doesn't have the "total picture" before making her decision — the future is unknown. We don't know where the Lord will lead us or how the Lord will use us. In faith a lifelong commitment is made. *Spiritual growth results when the believer learns to personalize self-discipline by affirming his decision daily to follow where Jesus leads.* I never knew God would one day use me to write a book, but I am grateful I followed Him in faith.

In Luke 9:23-25, Jesus described the steps necessary to follow Him. First, we must make the decision to "come after" Him, to accept Him. This is a personal choice reflecting a sincere desire to be a Christian. Next, He said that we must "deny" ourselves or give up selfish ambitions. Our own aspirations are to be replaced by His divine plans. Then, we are to "follow" Him in faith all the days of our lives. What a big decision! But what a blessed hope!

Have you made the personal decision to accept Jesus as Savior and follow Him as Lord? Your personal decision is the first step. You must make a sincere, genuine commitment. Only then will you be able to deny self and follow Him in faith. The choices we must face in our lives will result in a daily affirmation of commitment, if we are truly following Him. Remember, Jesus said, "Come after Me . . . deny your self . . . follow Me."

Genuine Decision

Jesus has issued an invitation to all people to "come after me" — to accept Him as Savior and serve Him as Lord. The same invitation extended to His disciples is offered to you and me. You, too, can accept Jesus. As a young girl, I heard my father faithfully proclaim in his sermons the invitation of Jesus. The Holy Spirit began to instill in me a desire to accept Jesus as Savior. Though I didn't fully understand doctrines and though I could not know the future, at six years of age, I made a genuine commitment to Jesus Christ in faith, publicly professing that faith and submitting myself to believer's baptism. My initial decision has been reaffirmed daily as I serve Jesus as Lord.

When Chuck asked me to marry him, I knew I wanted to say yes because I loved him. Though the future was unknown, I wanted to make a commitment to him. In the beautiful setting of a small chapel in Waco, Texas, I accepted in faith his proposal of marriage. I confirmed my response before a large gathering of people when we were married in the First Baptist Church of New Orleans on Friday, June 21, 1974. My decision to marry Chuck has been reaffirmed daily during these eighteen years. The commitment to marriage is much like the commitment to salvation. A conscious decision begins the lifelong commitment. It must be a sincere, genuine choice if the commitment is to last.

Our wedding service included what is commonly called the "Ruth ceremony." While the minister read from the first chapter of the book of Ruth, Chuck and I lit the single candle symbolizing that our two lives were becoming one life. What a beautiful experience! The Old Testament writer captured Ruth's complete commitment to Naomi in these words:

> But Ruth replied, "Don't urge me to leave you or turn back from you. Where you go I will go, and where you stay I will stay. Your people will be my people and your God my God. Where you die I will die, and there I will be buried. May the Lord deal with me, be it ever so severely, if anything but death separates you and me" (Ruth 1:16,17).

Ruth chose to accept Naomi's lifestyle. She gave up her own life and family to follow Naomi's life and family. Her decision was genuine, and it required sacrifice and lifelong commitment.

Our pastor, Dr. Roger Freeman, preached a sermon about the sevenfold commitment of Ruth. His text was this moving passage. He challenged the church to make a similar commitment to Christ. In his message, he described each choice made by Ruth. She told Naomi: (1) I will never leave you, (2) I will go with you, (3) I will live with you, (4) I will adopt your people, (5) I will worship your God, (6) I will die where you die, and (7) I will be buried where you are buried. Ruth was sincere in her commitment to Naomi, her mother-in-law. Are you sincere in your commitment to Jesus

Christ, your Savior? Salvation and marriage demand similar decisions of sacrifice and commitment.

When I began my quest for self-control, I made a sincere, genuine decision to do so. I had started diets many times before, but the decision had not been sincere. I often decided to diet before a physical check-up so my doctor wouldn't fuss at me for gaining weight. Or I began to diet before attending a class reunion so my friends wouldn't notice my change in size. I had many good motivations for losing weight but not a sincere desire for gaining self-control. Once I made a genuine decision, I was able to begin the journey through discipline.

Immediately after he completed his doctoral work, my husband, Chuck, was asked to teach at the New Orleans Baptist Theological Seminary. The offer baffled him. He had envisioned other plans for his future. It was a major, life-changing decision only he could make. I knew he would be an excellent teacher. Others felt confident in his ability to teach students preparing for ministry. God seemed to be opening a new door in a different direction. But Chuck alone had to make the final decision and accept God's redirection of his life if he was to be happy and fulfilled in his work. After much agony and soul-searching, he accepted the position as professor of evangelism. It was his decision — a genuine choice to follow God's will. Since that time, Chuck has often commented that it scares him to think how close he came to deliberately disobeying God. His initial decision to teach has required discipline but has provided many blessings.

You may have faced equally difficult decisions in your life. Maybe now God is offering you more personal discipline. If you have been convicted of your uncontrolled life, first you must decide to be disciplined. As a Christian, the decision to be disciplined and self-controlled means accepting the Holy Spirit's control of your life. The decision to accept His Spirit's control must be your choice. It must be a sincere, genuine decision to sacrifice yourself and follow Him in all areas of your life. No one else can make the decision for you. You alone must decide to accept Christ, and you alone must decide to be disciplined. Are you willing to make a sincere commitment?

Jesus told His disciples first to make a genuine choice. After that He asked them to deny themselves in order to follow Him. If you want to personalize discipline, you must accept Jesus, deny your-self, and follow Him. It is my prayer that you are willing to make that personal commitment to Jesus Christ.

Personal Change

The choice to accept Christ is not enough. Jesus said that com-mitment to Him also requires sacrifice of self—personal change. A believer must leave the past to pursue the future. The old life will be replaced by a new life. Personal goals and ambition will give way to God's plans and purpose. The Scripture says that we are to lay aside the old self with its evil practices and put on the new self which is being renewed in the image of God (Colossians 3:9,10). The re-sponsibility of the decision is yours alone. The reason for the deci-sion is the need for change. The object to be changed is you!

Leo Tolstoy, a great Russian writer, once said, "Everybody thinks of changing humanity, and nobody thinks of changing himself." Isn't that true? We can all think of others who need to change. Rarely do we recognize our own need to be transformed. In Mat-thew 7:3-5, Jesus reminded us that it is much easier for us to see faults in others than it is to see frailties in ourselves:

> "Why do you look at the speck of sawdust in your brother's eye and pay no attention to the plank in your own eye? How can you say to your brother, 'Let me take the speck out of your eye,' when all the time there is a plank in your own eye? You hypocrite, first take the plank out of your own eye, and then you will see clearly to remove the speck from your brother's eye."

We all tend to be hypocrites, seeing the faults in others while un-aware of our own failings. Change yourself first, then you will be able to encourage change in others.

Marriage, again, provides a classic example. A woman falls in love with a man, liking everything about him. However, as a wife, she immediately tries to change everything she once loved about him. The words "I do" (take you as my husband) become "I will" (change you into the man of my dreams). We are quick to force change on our husbands but not as quick to change ourselves.

As an eager young bride, I quickly learned there are some things about Chuck that I will never change. (I'm sure that you've learned a similar lesson about your husband!) I will never be able to change the way he squeezes the toothpaste, the way he eats his spaghetti, or the way he wakes up happy. He will always do those things! *What I can change is the way I respond.* I can buy two tubes of toothpaste, give him a spoon, and smile back in the morning. My focus needs to be on me. I can change myself, but I cannot force change on others.

Jesus told us to focus on ourselves. He told Martha, during a visit in Bethany, to worry about herself. While Martha was busy making preparations for Jesus, her sister Mary was listening to the words of Jesus. I relate to Martha, who complained to Jesus about her idle sister. She wanted Mary to change her behavior. She didn't give a thought to changing her own actions. Jesus told Martha to focus on her one priority — to change herself. "'Martha, Martha,' the Lord answered, 'you are worried and upset about many things, but only one thing is needed. Mary has chosen what is better, and it will not be taken away from her'" (Luke 10:41,42).

As the older of two girls, I often responded like Martha. While I was busy setting the table, Mitzi was talking on the telephone. While I was washing the dishes, my sister was reading a book. While I was studying, Mitzi was listening to music. My loud complaints often received a response similar to the one Jesus offered to Martha. Mother would chide me, "Rhonda, worry about yourself; don't worry about your sister." I needed to follow the advice of Jesus and change my own behavior. I tried to obey my mother's instructions and focus on myself.

In order to lead a Christian life, a believer must make a genuine decision and a personal change. A deliberate choice is made to accept Jesus as Savior, and a sincere commitment is made to change one's self. Once those steps have been taken, a believer can truly follow Christ. Self-control is necessary throughout the process. Specific steps must be taken to grow spiritually. It is my prayer that you will seek to personalize your discipline!

Total Commitment

Jesus continued giving His instructions to the disciples: "After you have accepted Me and agreed to deny self, then you must follow Me." To follow in faith is often frightening. You must be willing to place your life totally in the hands of God, even though you don't know the outcome. The practice of faith makes you feel both helpless and hopeful. While you abandon your own powers, you accept

His supernatural power. Christian faith begins when you trust Jesus with your life!

Several months ago I was suddenly confronted with the meaning of faith. I arrived by taxi early one morning at Victoria Station in London. I loaded all my bags on a cart and headed toward the train for the airport. When I couldn't find an elevator to go downstairs, I asked a janitor for help. He told me to push my long cart onto the escalator and release the handle. What a foolish idea! I knew the luggage cart was much too big and much too heavy for me to manage on an escalator. And I wasn't about to risk all my earthly possessions. But he insisted, "Push the cart down the escalator and let go." There was no one else around to reassure me, and my plane was to leave before long. So, finally, I stepped out in faith. I pushed the cart on the escalator; and as it moved down, I released the handle. My heart raced. I was worried to death. But do you know what happened? The escalator steps flattened out to hold my cart and my luggage was safely carried down. The escalator was specially designed to hold luggage carts. However, the escalator could have never worked for my cart if I had not given it a chance. I often wonder how many times my lack of faith has limited God's power to work.

God offers us salvation as a free gift if we will just accept it by faith. He gives us the gift because of His grace. We must receive it in faith. We cannot experience the power of God in our lives if we don't first accept Him by faith and then follow Him in faith. We don't know how His power works, just as I didn't know how the escalator worked, until we give Him our hearts. But in faith, we can follow Him.

Specific action must be taken if you are to follow Christ. A Christian should set goals and clarify objectives for godly living. Self-discipline is necessary to accomplish these goals. Immature, carnal believers have no spiritual goals. Their lives just unfold daily without a purpose. Mature, godly believers have specific, spiritual goals. Their lives are filled with activities that accomplish their purpose of becoming more like Christ. Reasonable goals are needed for spiritual growth.

Let's consider what we mean by "goal." A goal is simply a target for our behavior. It is a specific aim towards which an endeavor is directed. A goal is not a desire. JoAnn Leavell contrasted the difference between a goal and a desire in her book, *Don't Miss the Blessing*. She stated, "A goal is something I want which I can control. A desire is something I want which I *cannot* control. A wish, on the other hand, is a desire without any subsequent effort" (page 193). God would have us set reasonable goals for spiritual maturity.

My personal tendency is to make wishes rather than to set goals. I wish for many things in my life: "I wish I could lose weight." "I wish I had more money." "I wish I had more time to relax." Most of those statements are desires without any subsequent effort. *No change in behavior takes place when wishes are made.* A wish depends on mere luck, while a goal depends on hard work. I realized that I could change my undesired behaviors when I set specific goals. What I need to say is: "I will lose ten pounds." "I will save some money." "I will budget my time."

As you follow Christ, you should have goals that challenge you to grow. You need personal goals in all areas of your life: spiritual, mental, physical, family, social, and financial. Work in all areas ensures growth in all areas. Following Jesus requires total commitment and unlimited effort. His disciples learned this truth as they assisted in His ministry. We learn this lesson when we commit our priorities to Him.

Someone once said that he who aims at nothing hits it every time. Perhaps your spiritual life has been unproductive because you have been aiming at nothing. I want to share some personal principles that help me define my goals and achieve my objectives. It is very important to depend on God's power for guidance. While it has been said that success comes by "aspiration, inspiration, and perspiration," as Christians we receive the desire, discipline, and determination from God. The Lord has used these general guidelines to help me:

1. *Start simply.* Pick a fairly easy initial goal. Early success is a real encouragement.
2. *Be specific.* Don't set vague, general goals. You are more likely to accomplish specific, well-defined goals.
3. *Be realistic.* Try to identify goals that are within your reach. Break larger goals into smaller ones which can be achieved in a reasonable period of time.
4. *Be decisive.* Once you have made the decision to do something, do it. Indecision wastes a lot of time.

5. *Learn to say no.* When an activity doesn't help you accomplish one of your goals, don't do it. Say no to others in a gentle but firm way.

6. *Check your progress regularly.* It is helpful to monitor your progress periodically. If progress is minimal, you may need to reassess your goals.

7. *Revise your goals as needed.* There may be factors beyond your control that force you to revise your goals. Be flexible when your initial plans must change.

8. *Reward your accomplishments.* Don't forget to praise yourself when you complete a goal. Positive rewards will keep you working.

Because of my professional training, I am a believer in behavior modification. In my clinical work, I give tangible rewards to my patients as they accomplish goals. A happy face or a "scratch and sniff sticker" is a great reward for success. It is also a wonderful incentive for hard work. I use behavior modification principles on myself as well. A tangible reward is positive reinforcement for me. I altered my type of reward as I started to control my eating. Food rewards were replaced with non-edible rewards. I work very hard now for a bubble bath, a good magazine, or a phone call.

Jesus wants us to be disciplined. He wants us to accept Him, deny self, and follow Him. He wants us to use His divine instruction and some practical advice to set realistic goals for a disciplined life. If we are not disciplined, God's Word says we are disobedient, discouraged, and dysfunctional. "Like a city whose walls are broken down is a man who lacks self-control" (Proverbs 25:28).

Have you ever seen the ruins of an ancient city or a medieval castle? If the structure is not properly maintained, it will crumble. While fragile ruins inspire awe, they also indicate weakness. Lack of maintenance leads to gradual break-down. God's Word warns us that lack of discipline leads to destruction. The Christian who cannot control his heart and life will end in ruins, like an ancient city. Don't allow yourself to fall apart because of your lack of discipline!

Our challenge as believers is to personalize discipline — to practice control in our own lives. Ask yourself if you have obeyed Jesus in your initial commitment and your daily self-control. Have you made a definite decision to accept Christ? Have you focused your mind on changing yourself? Have you committed your life to following Christ? If your answers are yes, then you can pray this prayer of commitment with me: "Lord, I will come after You, I will deny myself, and I will follow You." When you have taken these steps, you have personalized discipline.

BIBLICAL STUDY

Read the message of Jesus to His disciples in Luke 9:23-25. Then honestly answer for yourself the question Jesus asks in verse 25: What does a man profit if he gains the whole world, but loses his soul? Write your response in the space provided.

PERSONAL APPLICATION

1. Have you made a genuine decision to accept Jesus Christ? If you can say yes with confidence, write your personal testimony below. If you must answer no, then read John 3:16 as you consider this important decision.

2. The only person you can successfully change is yourself. Think of several ways you need to change. List below at least three of your behaviors and describe ways you can change them.

3. On a scale from 1 to 10 (1 is the lowest and 10 is the highest), rate yourself in the space provided as a follower of Jesus. Ask God to help you improve in your areas of weakness.

I am faithful. _____

I am unselfish. _____

I am obedient. _____

Dear Lord,
I accept You as Savior, I deny myself as ruler, and I follow You as Lord. Help me to grow closer to You as I personalize discipline in my life.

Amen

CHAPTER 9

Perseverance and Discipline
(Discipline for a Lifetime)

For this very reason, make every effort to add to your faith goodness; and to goodness, knowledge; and to knowledge, self-control; and to self-control, *perseverance*; and to *perseverance*, godliness; and to godliness, brotherly kindness; and to brotherly kindness, love (2 Peter 1:5-7).

You should be convinced of the importance of self-discipline and convicted of any lack of discipline in your life. You have learned how to develop self-control in your life by adding God's supernatural power as well as the persuasive power of others to your own willpower. Once you personalize discipline in your life, you can begin to gain control of all areas of your life. Now it's time to learn the lesson that will make personal discipline last for a lifetime. *The key to maintaining a disciplined life is perseverance.*

While the word "perseverance" may seem cold and impersonal, its meaning should be warm and personal. A study from secular and biblical standpoints has endeared this word to me. Webster's dictionary defines perseverance as "continued, patient effort in spite of obstacles." Perseverance describes the character of one who is determined, persistent, and stubborn. *Perseverance is essential for success and happiness in life.* In order to accomplish goals, one must continue diligently along a definite course and remain focused in spite of obstacles. Stick with it! Don't give up! Don't let anything stop you! These attitudes are essential for perseverance.

I learned my greatest lesson in perseverance during the three years I worked on my doctorate. The learning process was painful at times, but the practice of perseverance made a permanent impact on my life. While working full time, I attended classes in the evening and wrote papers during the weekend. The end seemed so far away. But I knew God wanted me to complete my degree. He

had opened all the doors for my education, now I had to do my part
— persevere — even when I was tired and frustrated. Chuck and I
often say a doctorate is not a measure of intelligence; it is an award
for perseverance! Many of our friends began doctoral studies but
failed to complete them because they just didn't stick with it. Many
doctoral students complete all their classes, but never finish their
dissertations. They lack perseverance. Without perseverance, you
will fall short of many goals in life.

The Bible teaches us about perseverance. Scripture encourages
us to be steadfast, to continue growing, and to remain faithful.
Many New Testament passages include perseverance as a godly
trait of faithful Christians. *Unger's Bible Dictionary* defines perseverance as "the duty and privilege of a Christian to continue steadfastly in obedience and fidelity to Christ — not in order to inherit
eternal life but to demonstrate love and gratitude to Christ for His
great salvation." While constant obedience and a righteous life are
not necessary for salvation, they are evidences of salvation. God rewards His children for their perseverance through trials.

In order to maintain personal discipline in your life, you must
persevere. You must keep practicing self-control. You must continue to endure in spite of obstacles. You must remain steadfast in
purpose. You must stay on course, always trusting Jesus to give you
directions. Don't settle for fleeting success, but keep striving for
your best. As Helen Keller said, "We can do anything we want to do
if we stick with it long enough." God's Word teaches us that patience, persistence, and permanence are important aspects of
perseverance.

Patience

One of the most difficult concepts for many new Christians to
grasp is that God's children are not exempt from suffering. While
most of us realize that life is filled with disappointments and hardships, we want our faith to protect us from personal pain. Although
faith in the Lord and confidence in His power help us overcome
obstacles, Christians do experience sorrow and hurt. The patience
to endure our adversities comes through self-discipline and
perseverance.

Patience is a virtue many of us don't possess! Committing our lives to the Lord and practicing self-control will help us become patient and strong. The word "patience" actually means the ability to endure without complaint or to bear suffering with calmness and self-control. Many of us manage to endure, but not without loud complaints. I must confess to this weakness.

In my work with children, I need to be patient and calm as they learn lessons about life for themselves. Their behaviors and attitudes often test my patience, but I try very hard to understand their logic and to allow their inquiries. I find I have much more patience with children than I do with myself or other adults. Why? Because I make an intentional commitment to be patient with children. I also need to make this deliberate commitment with adults. God teaches us so much as we practice patience with others.

It has always been hard for me to endure without complaint. When I finally muster up enough strength to be patient, I can rarely be strong and silent at the same time. Maybe you can identify with this situation. Each time I went on a diet, I made everyone around me miserable. If I was denied the pleasures of eating, then I wanted to deny others their pleasures as well. Perhaps I should have worn a sandwich sign saying, "Beware of Dieter!" God helped me learn self-control and silence. He has taught me patience with myself and others.

A colleague at work has a very moody temperament. While she is a dear friend and a caring professional, she has her days. When she is angry or tired, she makes sure that everyone knows it. While it is impossible to predict her moods, it is always easy to know where she stands. She is very transparent and very explosive. The rest of us in the office have jokingly suggested that we "put out flares" to warn others of her bad mood. By nature, humans share their misery.

In our quest for divine discipline, Christians must be patient to endure suffering. We learn this lesson best from Jesus Christ, our model for godly living. In Hebrews 12:1-3, we are reminded to endure hardships, avoid sin, and persevere in life just as Jesus did. "Let us fix our eyes on Jesus, the author and perfecter of our faith, who for the joy set before him endured the cross, scorning its shame, and sat down at the right hand of the throne of God" (verse 2). Jesus endured persecution and scorn. He suffered without shame or complaint. Though He had every reason to become disillusioned, He persevered in peace. Jesus has the power to enable us to persevere because He Himself persevered. If we follow His pattern, we will not grow tired or become discouraged.

Like our Lord, we will face obstacles and experience suffering. If we keep our eyes on Jesus, we can endure and grow. The road of life is filled with detours and potholes. We encounter many interruptions in our daily routine that are beyond our control. Practice patience when these unexpected disturbances come your way. Life is also filled with pain — sickness and suffering, death and divorce. Persevere in your faith and depend on God for strength during times of personal crisis. Your patience will help you endure the situation and your perseverance will help you grow personally and spiritually. Remember that perseverance is yours if you seek it from God (Matthew 7:7,8).

At this time our most direct access to the nearby interstate highway is blocked off due to construction. There are no caution signs to warn drivers of the detour. Since Chuck and I often drive "on automatic pilot" as we talk or think, we frequently find ourselves inconvenienced as we approach the forgotten detour. These unpleasant surprises are a real hassle. They are beyond our control. Life is filled with irritating detours which we are unable to predict. If we are patient, we can persevere — we can make it.

The Apostle Paul practiced patience in his suffering and perseverance in his faith. He evidenced spiritual maturity and unending joy despite his circumstances. In Romans 5:3,4, Paul challenged us as believers to "rejoice in our sufferings, because we know that suffering produces perseverance; perseverance, character; and character, hope." Scripture teaches us that we are not only to be patient as we face trials and persevere in our faith, but we are to do so joyfully (James 1:2-4). As Christians our secret of a happy life is our confidence that God will overcome if we persevere. Discipline yourself with patience to endure life's challenges.

Persistence

One who perseveres must be patient to endure hardships and persistent to achieve objectives. God desires for His children to have purpose in life and to remain focused on personal goals. The New Testament is filled with scriptures which encourage believers to follow Jesus in their daily lives. Paul is again an example of a disciple of Christ focused on Jesus. He urged fellow Christians to grow in their faith, to move toward the goal, and to claim the prize. Using the imagery of a track race, Paul described his spiritual pilgrimage:

> Not that I have already obtained all this, or have already been made perfect, but I press on to take hold of that for which Christ Jesus took hold of me. Brothers, I do not consider myself yet to have taken hold of it. But one thing I do: Forgetting what is behind and straining toward what is ahead, I press on toward the goal to win the prize for which God has called me heavenward in Christ Jesus (Philippians 3:12-14).

Paul the apostle sought to be steadfast. We, too, should persist in our purpose — to know God and to walk in His power.

A friend of mine recently made a comment that illustrates the impact of a persistent faith. He said, "I am much more impressed with the testimony of a person who has always walked with the Lord than one who after rebellion returns to the Lord." It is true. We often admire a person who has had a dramatic conversion after a very sinful life. A personal account of an addiction to drugs or sexual promiscuity before a miraculous rededication to the Lord brings tears to the eyes of Christians but it also causes doubt for many whose lives have not been so visibly changed. God rejoices in the salvation of broken lives. He also glories in the perseverance of the saints.

Do you have friends who have trouble sticking with a job or who move often? Some people seem very unsettled and unstable. They just don't stay committed for long periods of time. They give up when work becomes difficult or when life becomes challenging. While there are definitely times when God redirects our paths, He wants us to find His will for our lives where we are and keep doing it.

I'm grateful that Chuck and I have had fairly settled lives. We have lived in only two towns and four homes in eighteen years of marriage. In fact, we've lived in New Orleans for the last sixteen years. We have had time to cultivate meaningful relationships and build a solid foundation. I have held only three different jobs and have been in the present one for thirteen years. I always wanted to be a speech pathologist, and Chuck always felt called to the ministry. Christians can serve God more effectively when they invest their lives for the long haul.

If God wants us to be steadfast in purpose, then we must discipline ourselves daily. Jesus told His disciples to persist in following Him: "'If anyone would come after me, he must deny himself and take up his cross *daily* and follow me'" (Luke 9:23). We as Christians in search of divine discipline need to renew our commitment to the Lord daily. Dallas Willard in *The Spirit of the Disciplines* reminds us that discipline isn't instant when he states, "There is no quick fix . . . it is a process of great length and difficulty that engages all our own powers to their fullest extent over a long course of experience" (page 70). *Daily recommitment leads to lasting discipline.*

Persistence must be practiced in several areas of our lives. First, we must persist in our faith. Mature Christians are growing in their knowledge and understanding of the scriptures as well as their personal relationships with God. Spiritual maturity involves daily discipline. A person who fails to grow in his personal walk with the Lord remains a "babe in Christ." Those who persist in their faith become true men and women of God (1 Timothy 6:11,12; Romans 15:4-6). Brother Andrew, a medieval monk known for his close walk with God, reminded himself daily that he was in the presence of God. His disciplined life became a habit and the secret to his holy living.

Second, we must persist in obedience. Mature Christians obey the commandments of the Lord. While good works don't save us, they are the evidence of a saved life. God forgives us of any confessed sin, but He also wants us to be obedient and godly. Our society today is acutely aware of many highly visible Christians who stopped obeying God and started following self. Their personal disobedience led to intense public scrutiny and public humiliation. In Revelation 14:12, John concludes that the godly life "calls for patient endurance on the part of the saints who obey God's commandments and remain faithful to Jesus." Those who practice divine discipline will obey God's commandments, while those who lack discipline will disobey.

Third, we must persist in service. Mature Christians are busy serving the Lord. Christian service requires self-discipline and perseverance. God needs His children to do His work in the world. Even though He is capable of accomplishing His will in His own power, God chooses to use us as instruments in ministry. Christians are not only commanded to serve others. If they persevere in their service, they grow spiritually. In 1 Corinthians 15:58 the Apostle

Paul says: "Stand firm. Let nothing move you. Always give your-selves fully to the work of the Lord, because you know that your labor in the Lord is not in vain." Faithful servants of God persevere in service to others and are richly blessed by their work.

Jesus commended three of the seven churches in the book of Revelation for their perseverance. Although they had some prob-lems, these churches were praised because they persisted in faith, in obedience, and in service. Their perseverance pleased the Lord. John records that Jesus commended the church in Ephesus for their "'hard work and perseverance. . . . You have persevered and have endured hardships for my name, and have not grown weary'" (Revelation 2:2,3). The church in Thyatira was also commended for its deeds, love, faith, service, and perseverance. Jesus added that they were "'now doing more than (they) did at first'" (Revelation 2:19). Those followers of Christ who grew in faith and expanded their ministry demonstrated perseverance and persistence. The church in Philadelphia was promised God's deliverance because of their obedience and patience: "'Since you have kept my command to endure patiently, I will also keep you from the hour of trial that is going to come upon the whole world'" (Revelation 3:10). How did these people develop perseverance? When they did something good, they did it again. If we as Christians want to be praised by God, we must be patient while enduring hardships and remain persist-ent in purpose.

Permanence

Perseverance and discipline require patience and persistence if they are to last for a lifetime. They must also become permanent. When people ask me how I have kept the pounds off, I respond, "I have made permanent behavior changes that will last a lifetime." You see, any change in behavior will be lifelong only if the individ-ual makes the change permanent. You must recommit daily to self-control. You must keep on keeping on. You must stay on course, persevering in your discipline. A lifestyle of discipline requires per-severance. Spiritual commitment as well as physical fitness must be permanent priorities.

Most of us who have struggled with a weight problem realize that a diet is successful only if lifestyle behavioral changes are made and maintained. Every effective diet plan includes a maintenance program. The National Center for Health Statistics reports that the rate of regain on any weight-loss regime is 95 percent unless permanent changes in eating and exercise are made. The failure rate is high because most dieters do not persevere.

I followed the public progress of Oprah Winfrey's liquid diet in the late 1980s with great interest. (You may have, too!) Before her TV audience, she proudly displayed her sixty-seven-pound weight loss in a pair of skin-tight, size-ten jeans. Oprah has now become one of the most visible examples of "the pain of regain." Like the majority of all dieters, she was unable to keep the pounds off because she did not make lifestyle changes in her eating and exercise. I was interested in reading her thoughts on her inevitable failure. She failed to keep her ideal weight after she quit her diet group, discontinued her maintenance program, stopped her regular exercise, and opened a high-fat restaurant in Chicago where she often ate herself. Oprah readily admits that her very visible failure to keep the weight off was her greatest failure in life. Now she has adopted a new attitude about her weight, "I'm trying to find a way to live in a world with food without being controlled by it. What is the issue is getting healthy, getting fit and being strong."

No matter which behavior you are trying to control, you must persevere in order to make the change permanent. Spiritual discipline as well as physical discipline demands a lifestyle of commitment. Dieting seems to provide the best example of the importance of maintenance. In their ten-stage life plan for the body, mind, and soul, the authors of *Love Hunger* list a commitment to maintenance which includes daily prayer and devotional reading, daily support outside the family, daily group fellowship, daily physical exercise, daily relational survey, daily activity planning, and daily food planning (pages 182-184). The key to successful maintenance is *daily maintenance*. Jesus in Luke 9:23 said, "'If anyone would come after me, he must deny himself and take up his cross *daily* and follow me.'" If you want to make permanent changes in your physical, spiritual, or personal life, you must recommit yourself daily. When you do this, your new behavior will become a new lifestyle.

Unfortunately, maintenance isn't easy, and persistence doesn't come naturally to most of us. We must work at it. We must discipline ourselves to create a new lifestyle. My husband, Chuck, likes to say, "I have no trouble losing weight. My problem is, I keep finding it again."

That's precisely the problem for most of us. We regain our weight, we return to our sinful nature, and we resume our ungodly living. While a new lifestyle with permanent self-control is no simple matter, as Christians we can claim God's supernatural power to help us develop and maintain divine discipline. What a blessing!

Because perseverance isn't a natural behavior, we are all going to experience setbacks. That was a hard lesson for me to learn since I don't like to fail. Overweight all my life, I have been like a yo-yo with my weight going up and down. Can you identify with this experience? I often punished myself or felt like a failure if my diet wasn't a perfect success. I now realize that *lapses are the rule rather than the exception.* It is more common for people to fail in their attempts than to succeed. We must train ourselves to put our failures behind and move on toward success.

In their book, *The New Aerobics for Women,* Kenneth and Millie Cooper discuss the psychological motivators that keep people exercising. They encourage us to: "Perceive a lapse as a momentary interruption; do not see it as a failure forever. Forgive yourself and start again, whether it's for the second time or the twentieth" (page 79). That is good advice for physical fitness and spiritual discipline.

I have a tendency to fizzle out in my daily quiet time and in my daily exercise program. I start out with sincere intentions and a good plan, but I get busy and lose interest. There are so many distractions in life and so many other good things to do. As maturing, obedient Christians we must persevere in our self-discipline in order to make permanent changes in our lives. We must start again to use our own personal willpower, God's supernatural power, and the persuasive powers of others to control the uncontrolled areas of our lives. And remember, you can already claim the victory and relish the rewards of permanent divine discipline.

God still wants to use us even when we stumble, but He can't if we refuse to get up. Charles Swindoll discusses forgiveness and redirection in his book, *Starting Over.* He concludes that success is not measured as much by the absence of failure as by the willingness to start over. Swindoll states, "The person who succeeds is not the one who holds back, fearing failure, nor the one who never fails . . . but rather the one who moves on in spite of failure" (page 26). The greatest failures in the eyes of the world can become the truest successes by the power of God when we move out in faith.

It is a great consolation to know that God forgives us when we fail and helps us start again. The prophet Jonah learned that lesson when God gave him a second chance to preach in Ninevah. At first Jonah tried to run away from God. After God disciplined him with three days in the belly of a great fish, Jonah again cried out to God. Jonah 3:1 says that "the word of the Lord came to Jonah a second time." The reluctant prophet was allowed to start over. He became an effective spokesman for God. If you feel trapped in a life that is as confining to you as the belly of a fish was to Jonah, do what he did. Stop trying to run from God. Cry out to Him for forgiveness and help. Our God is the God of second chances!

The scriptures offer help as we try to maintain self-control. If you want to persist in your faith, "make every effort to add to your faith goodness; and to goodness, knowledge; and to knowledge, self-control; and to self-control, perseverance; and to perseverance, godliness; and to godliness, brotherly kindness; and to brotherly kindness, love" (2 Peter 1:5-7). Faith alone is enough to guarantee salvation, but faith alone is not enough to assure lasting satisfaction. As Christians we must keep growing. We must persevere in godly living. If we practice developing and maintaining godly virtues daily, they will become a habit — a good habit.

What an overwhelming challenge! But, what an unspeakable joy! As disciplined Christians seeking permanent righteous living, we must be patient to endure hardships, to persist in our faith, and to persevere daily. This acronym may help you remember what we have learned about perseverance.

P ersistence

E ndurance

R enewal

S teadfastness

E xcellence

V itality

E ffort

R ecommitment

E nthusiasm

BIBLICAL STUDY

Read 2 Peter 1:5-7 in several Bible translations. List below the seven qualities that Christians should add to their faith. Briefly describe each virtue in your own words.

1.

2.

3.

4.

5.

6.

7.

PERSONAL APPLICATION

1. Of the seven qualities listed above, which two do you possess in the greatest measure? _____ and _____ . Which two do you need to develop? _____ and _____ . Discuss below how you can develop these qualities in your life.

2. Ask yourself this probing question: "How well have I persisted in my faith, my obedience, and my service?" Be honest, then seek God's forgiveness and make a new promise to persevere. Write your prayer of recommitment below.

3. In what areas of self-discipline have you persevered? Fill in the blanks below to record specific activities or attitudes you have maintained.

daily _____

daily _____

daily _____

Thank God for His power to sustain you and your determination to stick with it.

Dear Lord,

It is so hard to stay disciplined. Please help me to be patient to endure hardships and to be persistent in life so my changes will be truly permanent lifetime changes.

Amen

CHAPTER 10

Promises of Discipline
(Rewards of Self-Discipline)

Everyone who competes in the games exercises self-control in all things. They then do it to receive a perishable wreath, but we an imperishable (1 Corinthians 9:25 NAS).

The assurance of a promise doesn't seem as permanent today as it did in the past. In our society, the vows of marriage are frequently broken and contracts are often severed. We don't seem committed to keep our promises. We have adopted an attitude that relationships don't always last and agreements can easily be altered on personal whim. In fact, we generally accept that "promises are made to be broken."

It is a great comfort for Christians to know without doubt that God's promises are never broken. The Bible is filled with precious promises from God to His children. Biblical scholars have identified more than 30,000 promises in God's Word — promises of protection, comfort, guidance, forgiveness, and love. The precious promises of God can be claimed by anyone who trusts Him for salvation and follows Him in godly living. God's promises are easily understood and always fulfilled. We are the benefactors of God's promises not because of our worth or works but because of His unconditional love.

If you are not experiencing the promises of God in your life, you may be wondering why. In order to receive God's promises, a person must repent of sins, follow in faith, and persevere in obedience. The Old Testament includes several conditional promises made by God to His children. These are not promises with strings attached, but agreements requiring action. In 2 Chronicles 7:14, the Lord said: "'If my people, who are called by my name, will humble themselves and pray and seek my face and turn from their wicked ways, then will I hear from heaven and will forgive their sin and will heal their land.'" If we Christians will turn to God, repent of our sins, and live godly lives, then God will hear our prayers, forgive our sins, and restore our lives.

God's promises to disciplined believers come in the form of rewards now here on earth and later for all eternity in heaven. While our motivation for self-control in our daily lives should not be recognition from God, our obedience is rewarded by His blessings. Let these promises of strength and hope give you the stamina and courage to persevere in your personal discipline.

Past Blessing

Aren't you grateful for God's many blessings in your life? As I reflect on my own life, I am overwhelmed with gratitude for all God has done for me. I thank Him daily for the blessings of health, provision, marriage, family, work, and on and on. He has been *so* good to me. I feel so undeserving of His generous gifts and unending love.

I have recently noticed in my prayer journal that I have already filled more pages on "giving thanks" than on "requests for self" or "petitions for others." That's as it should be — we need to spend more time in prayer thanking God for His blessings than asking for His help. Our hearts should overflow with praise to Him. The psalmist David offered praise to the Lord in Psalm 92, one of my favorite songs of praise:

> It is good to praise the Lord and make music to your name, O Most High, to proclaim your love in the morning and your faithfulness at night. . . . For you make me glad by your deeds, O Lord; I sing for joy at the works of your hands. How great are your works, O Lord, how profound your thoughts! . . . You, O Lord, are exalted forever (verses 1-8).

Have you ever asked yourself these questions: Why has God been so good to me? Why has God chosen to bless my life so abundantly? Don't feel alone if you have asked these questions. Most Christians have asked them; I have, too. My understanding of the answers to these questions is found in God's Word. God promises abundant life to those who follow Him (John 10:10). He promises blessings to all who obey His commandments and serve Him faithfully (2 Peter 1:4). Perhaps you do not feel abundantly blessed right now. The hardships and suffering of life sometimes obscure God's blessings. Remain confident that God will keep His promise of blessings. *Disciplined, godly living is rewarded by blessings here on earth as well as crowns of glory in heaven.*

God's blessings come to us in many different shapes and forms. Because God knows each of us intimately, He tailor-makes our personal blessings. As you reflect upon past blessings in your life, you will undoubtedly think of family and friends as well as experiences and opportunities. God has chosen to bless your life through people and things because of your faithfulness in following Him. Don't miss out on these blessings due to unnecessary humility; enjoy them as a result of God's unselfish love.

When I reflect on the blessings of my life, I see that they have come in various forms. My greatest blessing in life is, without doubt, my precious husband, Chuck. He is a tremendous blessing that I will enjoy for the rest of my life. I am so grateful for his love, tenderness, and encouragement which are ongoing blessings. God has also given me small blessings as I meet wonderful new Christian friends in my ministry travels. Although I am with them only briefly, they bless my life. Many of the blessings of my life are people. I also experience blessings from God in the form of things. A beautiful flower is such a blessing, especially on a busy, rainy day. The majesty of the Canadian Rockies was a recent blessing to me. The beauty of God's creation coupled with a week of relaxation was a true blessing. Aren't we glad God's blessings have our names written on them?

The clearest image in the Bible of God's blessings for His children is found in the description of the fruit of the Spirit. Paul lists the fruit of the Holy Spirit in Galatians 5:22,23: love, joy, peace, patience, kindness, goodness, faithfulness, gentleness, and self-control. These godly virtues are characteristic of a growing Christian life. If you practice self-control in all areas of your life, God promises you the fruit of the Spirit. Who doesn't want to experience love, joy, and peace?

Hebrews 12:11 promises "a harvest of righteousness and peace" for those who are trained by discipline. The fruit of a righteous life is available to all believers who persist in obedience to God's will. Our lives will be blessed abundantly as we make any necessary sacrifices for the sake of self-discipline.

Disciplined, godly living will be rewarded by the fruit of the Spirit as you relate to God — love, joy, and peace. God will continue to bless your life with these three Christian graces as you grow in your knowledge of His Word and walk in the confidence of your faith.

Love from God is the unselfish, sacrificial kind of love that helps us love even those who hate us. If Christ lives in you, your life will be filled with love. *Joy* that indwells the heart of a believer is true happiness and delight that overcomes his natural feelings. When Christ controls your life, you will experience joy daily as you recognize His work in your world. *Peace*, the condition of well-being and tranquillity, is promised to believers despite their circumstances. You can have peace of heart and peace with others. These blessings are yours as you develop divine discipline.

I am so grateful for God's gifts of love, joy, and peace in my own life. I know I would not experience these emotions to such a degree without His gracious mercy. He showers me with these blessings even when life in the real world seems to be caving in. During times of personal crisis, I feel God's love, joy, and peace lifting me up. My circumstances don't control my feelings toward God. Years of deep love and devotion to God prepare me to face the problems and assure me of God's promises to sustain me. Since I have sown seeds of faith, I am able to reap the harvest of righteousness.

Disciplined, godly living will also be rewarded by the fruit of the Spirit as you relate to others — patience, kindness, and goodness. When a Christian's relationship with God is right, his relationships with others will be right. It is impossible to experience love, joy, and peace with God, if you don't express patience, kindness, and goodness toward your fellowman.

Patience or longsuffering is a by-product of our relationship with God and an essential ingredient in our relationships with our neighbors. Human patience is limited, but God's longsuffering is limitless. It is the patience of God that allows us to persevere in our love for God, others, and self. *Kindness* (gentleness in the *King James Version*) is an important attribute of God and virtue of His children. Tenderness and understanding toward others demonstrate our faith and allow our service. *Goodness* was a favorite word of the Apostle Paul, who put his love for others into action. True goodness is revealed in what we say and what we do. Goodness is not only an internal trait, but also an external behavior. Kindness is built on the virtue of patience and is the foundation for the quality of goodness. These additional virtues are yours as you maintain divine discipline.

A friend at work once told me of a cute experience she had with her children. One Saturday they stopped at a church in their neighborhood for the youth car wash. Her oldest son commented, "These people all sound like Mrs. Rhonda." She laughed and responded, "Yes, that's the way all Christians talk. They're all very nice." I thanked God for giving me a spirit of patience, kindness, and goodness toward others evidenced naturally by me even when I didn't feel great. A disciplined walk with the Lord will be reflected in your relationship with others even though you are unaware of it.

Finally, disciplined, godly living will be rewarded by the fruit of the Spirit as you relate to self — faithfulness, gentleness, and self-control. While the first three fruit are upward (God), the next three are outward (others), and these last three are inward (self).

Faithfulness is the quality which marks one who can be trusted to carry out responsibilities. It takes self-discipline to continue to serve without faltering. *Gentleness* (or meekness) does not imply weakness, but instead it exhibits an inner strength because it is "not I but Christ in me." Meekness demands submission of self in order to serve God and others. *Self-control* is also translated as temperance. It is the power to take hold of self and master personal passions. *Self-control is the inner strength which gives us victory over fleshly desires and selfish ambitions.* Self-control is essential to Christian maturity. It is an evidence of spiritual growth. The crowning fruit of the Spirit are yours as you persevere in divine discipline.

It is so easy for me to find fault with myself. I look in the mirror and find all the flaws — crow's feet, midriff bulge, saddlebags. I quickly remind myself that God made me and "He makes no mistakes." He created me uniquely for a specific purpose — nothing about me was an accident. If I truly believe this, then I must lovingly accept myself as prescribed by the Creator. As I study God's Word and learn of His nature, I become aware of His plan for my life and His rewards for my obedience. My daily discipline helps me love myself and enjoy the blessings in my life.

Several years ago I personally learned a lesson that illustrates the biblical teaching that "you reap what you sow." I love flowers, especially bright-colored tulips and daffodils. So, each winter I meticulously plant bulbs in order to enjoy beautiful blossoms in the spring. You can imagine my frustration when months after I planted dozens of bulbs, not even a small sprout had emerged from the ground. Impatient, I decided to dig down in the dirt to see what the problem might be. I was astonished to find pecans buried in my flower planters. The pesky squirrels in my backyard had eaten four dozen tulip bulbs and replaced them with their own treasure — pecans! I was furious! I had no beautiful flowers that spring. I learned an important lesson — you reap what you sow. Flowers don't grow when pecans are planted. You only have beautiful flowers when bulbs are planted and tended. That is also true in life. You only harvest the fruit of God's Spirit when you sow seeds of faith and righteousness.

In Galatians 5, Paul pictures a beautiful tree bearing nine precious fruit. You will enjoy the fruit only when you diligently tend the tree. The tree of your life needs daily watering and continual pruning if it is to grow and flourish. Without discipline and perseverance in your spiritual life, you will not produce or reap the fruit of the Spirit. God's promised harvest has brought you past blessings, it is bringing you present freedom, and it will bring you future hope.

Present Freedom

While it is natural to think of bondage and sacrifice when you hear the word "discipline," actually the ultimate result of discipline is freedom. Discipline is not a "bad word." The disciplined life yields freedom in Christ. No longer do you experience bondage to people or things. Your schedule no longer holds you captive; you have time to do the things you enjoy. *The commitment of your heart frees you from the restriction of rules.* There is freedom in self-control!

I have always felt imprisoned while on a diet. Diet plans with prescribed meals and rigid portions always frustrate me. I feel defeated almost before I begin. When God taught me self-control in eating, I found freedom to eat healthy foods. My attitude changed. The same negative reaction occurs in life when we are forced to obey rules. If our hearts know the spirit of the law, our actions will follow. Godly living will flow spontaneously from a committed heart.

Let's see what the Bible teaches about freedom. Freedom is at the very core of the gospel and godly living. Galatians 5:1 informs believers that "it is for freedom that Christ has set us free." Jesus Christ wants us to be free. His death on the cross guaranteed our freedom from the penalty of sin. His presence with us gives us freedom in our daily lives. God has called *all* believers to freedom; His call is universal (Galatians 5:13). This freedom is not a license to disobey; it is a freedom to trust God in love.

In his commentary on Galatians, John MacArthur discusses these four purposes of freedom: (1) to oppose the flesh, (2) to serve others, (3) to fulfill God's moral law, and (4) to avoid harming others. Christ's sacrificial death freed us from the legalism of the law. His Spirit's presence in our lives empowers us to pursue true freedom. Self-control is essential to the purposes of freedom. Without divine discipline, we will be unable to resist sin, serve our fellowman, obey God's law, and love others. It is self-discipline that makes way for freedom.

Freedom, or release from obligation, comes through simple faith in God and commitment to His will for our life. In salvation, we are assured of our destiny and exempted from obeying the "letter of the law." We don't have to measure up to God's standards to be saved. Christ died to free us from that impossible feat. Instead, our trust in God gives us the sincere desire and the actual ability to live righteously.

Aren't you glad you don't have to earn freedom? Freedom is a reward of your salvation and godly living. Richard Foster briefly mentioned the reward of freedom in his book, *Celebration of Discipline*. He said, "Every discipline has its corresponding freedom and the purpose of the disciplines is freedom. Our aim is the freedom, not the discipline" (page 193). It is true that most of us seek freedom at any cost. Unfortunately, we are not often willing to pay the price of discipline to obtain freedom. Our goal is divine discipline. Our reward is freedom.

The area of my physical life requiring the most discipline is exercise. I can maintain healthy eating because healthy eating takes no more time than unhealthy eating. It is very hard, however, for me to schedule regular exercise. I start walking for thirty minutes three times a week, then the weather gets bad and the days get busy and I stop. I start exercising again. I go to aerobics twice each week then I go on vacation and the days get busy and I stop. Again I start to exercise by riding my stationary bicycle each weeknight. Soon I become bored and the days get busy and I stop. What's missing? My discipline and perseverance. I know that if I make the necessary sacrifices to exercise regularly, I will feel better — that's freedom. If my aim is discipline in exercise, then my reward will be freedom in health.

In her book, *The Christian's Secret of a Happy Life*, Hannah Whitall Smith talks about the promises of discipline as "chariots of God." She believes that God sends gifts to strengthen and delight the souls of those who are weary from the demands of a disciplined life. Personal discipline does promise freedom in salvation and godly living. Smith says:

> The man who lives by the power of an inward righteous nature is not under bondage to the outward law of righteousness; but he who is restrained by the outward law alone, without the inward restraint of a righteous nature, is a slave to the law. The one fulfills the law in his soul, and is therefore free. The other rebels against the law in his soul, and is therefore bound (page 109).

Paul further explains this freedom in the Lord in Romans 6:22. He writes that as believers we "have been set free from sin and have become slaves to God." Our freedom through salvation requires perseverance in holiness. Divine discipline has been rewarded with past blessings and present freedom. God also promises us eternal life — our future hope.

Future Hope

I am glad that God's rewards for self-discipline are granted to us here on earth as well as later in heaven. It would be hard to wait to experience all of His precious promises. I am so inquisitive, especially about desirable things. God knows our impatient, curious natures and helps us persevere. However, He also pours out His blessings, giving us just a glimpse of the eternal rewards awaiting us in heaven. The eternal rewards are our future hope!

How can we receive rewards in heaven? To whom does God present eternal rewards? According to Scripture, there are some specific criteria. Those who live in the flesh will not receive heavenly rewards. Those who live in the Spirit will reap an eternal harvest. The Bible teaches that there are only two fields in which seed can be sown — the field of the flesh or the field of the Spirit. The flesh refers to selfish, uncontrolled, human living, while the Spirit describes unselfish, disciplined, godly living. The kind of harvest is determined by where and how the seed is planted. If you plant seeds of the flesh, you reap corruption and death. If you plant seeds of the Spirit, you reap joy and eternal life. Your future harvest is measured by where your present crop is planted.

Galatians 6:8,9 says:

> The one who sows to please his sinful nature, from that nature will reap destruction; the one who sows to please the Spirit, from the Spirit will reap eternal life. Let us not become weary in doing good, for at the proper time we will reap a harvest if we do not give up.

A sinful Christian reaps a harvest of pain and suffering now and a lack of rewards in eternity. A righteous Christian produces the fruit of the Spirit here on earth and gains eternal rewards. Divine discipline is essential. If you persevere in godly living, you will receive God's richest blessings forever.

While a believer who "sows to his own flesh" does not lose his salvation, that believer certainly loses the fruit of the Spirit. It is so sad to see Christians lose the joy of their salvation. While the unrighteous believer will still go to heaven, he will not experience God's blessings here on earth or His crowns of righteousness for all eternity. King David knew what it was like to lose the joy of his salvation. His sin separated him from God and stopped the harvest of the fruit. In Psalm 51, he cried out to God, "Restore to me the joy of your salvation" (verse 12). A sinful life produces temporary pleasures, but not eternal joy.

Those verses in Galatians remind us that the harvest comes "in due time." God's due time. If it were my time, it would be right now or even yesterday. But God knows when to bring the harvest. His timetable is perfect. God's seasons govern the ripeness of the crops. The omniscient Father knows the proper time to reward our faithfulness. He tells us to persevere in divine discipline until the harvest comes.

Paul not only persevered in the Lord's work, he reaped the harvest. He was blessed in his life because he never gave up, even when he became weary and his heart became heavy. That faithful apostle reaped the fruit of the Spirit in this life (1 Thessalonians 2:19) and the rewards for devoted service in eternal life (2 Timothy 4:7-8).

The great evangelist George Whitefield once wrote in his journal, "Lord, I am weary in your work, but not of your work." We, too, must not let our tired bodies cause tired spirits.

The choice of the harvest is yours. In which field will you sow seeds — the field of the flesh or the field of the Spirit? Which harvest will you reap — corruption or eternal life? It is my prayer that you will persevere in godliness so that you will receive earthly joy and heavenly rewards.

The Bible speaks of the "imperishable wreath" awarded to those who exercise self-control in all things (1 Corinthians 9:25 NAS). The "imperishable wreath" is a lasting recognition for dedicated living. Scripture also speaks of heavenly crowns, additional rewards for Christian service given out in heaven. A disciplined life merits crowns in glory.

The New Testament uses heavenly crowns to illustrate the eternal rewards given to faithful believers in heaven. Each reward is best understood within the context of its message. The following references describe those crowns.

1. the crown of life (James 1:12)
2. the crown of rejoicing (1 Thessalonians 2:19)
3. the crown of righteousness (2 Timothy 4:8)
4. the crown of glory (1 Peter 5:4)

James 1:12 discusses the crown of life: "Blessed is the man who perseveres under trial, because when he has stood the test, he will receive the crown of life that God has promised to those who love him." The crown of life is a prize of kingly glory worn by Christians who persevered in their faith through trials. While salvation is a free gift guaranteeing eternal life, the crown of life is earned by the believer for unwavering faith.

The crown of rejoicing is described in 1 Thessalonians 2:19: "For what is our hope, our joy, or the crown in which we will glory in the presence of the Lord Jesus Christ when he comes? Is it not you?" Paul praised the Christians at Thessalonica for believing and keeping the Word of God even in the face of persecution. He encouraged them to persevere in their faith and maintain discipline in their living so they would experience joy on earth and the crown of rejoicing in heaven.

The third reference mentions a crown of righteousness: "Now

there is in store for me the crown of righteousness, which the Lord, the righteous Judge, will award to me on that day — and not only to me, but also to all who have longed for his appearing" (2 Timothy 4:8). Paul himself anticipated his reward in heaven for godly living and dedicated service. Those who proclaim the gospel faithfully and await the return of Jesus eagerly will receive the crown of righteousness in heaven.

The last example of a heavenly crown is found in 1 Peter 5:4: "And when the Chief Shepherd appears, you will receive the crown of glory that will never fade away." An eternal crown of glory awaits all Christian leaders or undershepherds who feed their flock according to the will of God. Jesus Christ Himself will give glory to them for their lives of example and leadership. Heavenly crowns will be placed lovingly by our King of Glory on the heads of all believers who faithfully serve Him.

God's blessings here on earth are so thrilling. But, I also look forward to receiving the eternal rewards for my godly life and devoted service. I don't know how the heavenly crowns will look. I don't even know all that they represent. I am confident that God will reward my life in a manner beyond my comprehension. Right now, I must do my part to be disciplined in my daily life.

Are you planting seeds of righteousness to reap a harvest of blessing? If so, rejoice! You will know the joy and happiness of God's blessings on earth. You will experience freedom from the bondage of sin, and you will receive heavenly rewards for devoted service. If not, repent! Trust Jesus with your heart and develop divine discipline in your life. All believers who live out their faith each day have the assurance of salvation and eternal life.

On a recent trip to Edinburgh, Scotland, we visited the Holyrood Palace, the home of all Scottish royalty. A family abbey was built adjacent to the palace during the twelfth century. My husband, Chuck, enjoyed reading the tombstones in its cemetery. (That is natural for the son of an undertaker!) He discovered one epitaph that inspired us both. The inscription was directed to the reader — to all of us. Read its message thoughtfully:

> Be thou taught by this:
> To seek those riches which never can fail.
> And those pleasures
> Which are at God's right hand for evermore.

The gracious gift of God.
And to be enjoyed through faith
in Jesus Christ our Saviour.

As Christians, we should not be satisfied with our salvation. We should discipline ourselves to live godly lives and serve the Lord faithfully. Then we will receive those riches which never fail and those pleasures which last forever.

I am grateful for God's past blessing and His present freedom, and I look forward to His future hope. It will be joy unspeakable to spend all eternity in fellowship with the Father. My eighty-seven-year-old grandfather is a retired Methodist minister. He loves to talk about heaven. He looks forward to a reunion with God the Father, with his beloved wife, and with his precious mother. Granddaddy Harrington recently had a stroke which has left him paralyzed on the left side of his body. While in the hospital, he asked me to read aloud Revelation 4 and 5. The promise of those verses brought tears to his eyes (and mine) each time I read:

> After this I looked, and there before me was a door standing open in heaven. And the voice I had first heard speaking to me like a trumpet said, "Come up here, and I will show you what must take place after this." At once I was in the Spirit, and there before me was a throne in heaven (Revelation 4:1,2).

What a comfort and what a hope!

BIBLICAL STUDY

Read the following passages from Proverbs. What does each one teach about God's promises for disciplined living? Write a short answer in the space provided.

Proverbs 10:6: _____

Proverbs 10:25: _____

Proverbs 10:28: _____

Proverbs 11:8: _____

Proverbs 11:30: _____

PERSONAL APPLICATION

1. Recall some past blessings in your life. As you write them below, thank God for His generosity.

2. Look up the word "freedom" in the dictionary. What does it tell you about freedom that results from discipline. Express your feelings below.

3. What do you imagine when you think of heaven? What are the heavenly crowns you desire as your rewards for Christian service? Describe your future hope in the space provided.

Dear Lord,
Thank You for Your precious promises and for the rewards of a disciplined life — the past blessing, the present freedom, and the future hope. You are a great God!

Amen

CHAPTER 11

The Disciplines of Life
(Self-Control and Other Disciplines)

Discipline yourself for the purpose of godliness; for bodily discipline is only of little profit, but godliness is profitable for all things, since it holds promise for the present life and also for the life to come (1 Timothy 4:7,8 NAS).

What could be more heartbreaking than something that fails to grow or someone who never reaches full potential? A seedling that never matures into a beautiful plant or majestic tree. An intelligent, gifted person who lacks initiative. Many of us have special abilities we never develop. Our lack of self-determination limits our personal growth and spiritual maturity. Healthy growth requires discipline in every area of life.

In my professional career, I have worked on occasion with children who failed to grow physically or mentally. In such cases the infant's body doesn't grow properly as the child ages due to physical problems. While alert and aware, the baby does not gain weight or grow as it should. The lack of physical growth is life-threatening. A child with mental retardation grows physically but fails to advance intellectually. While the body reflects the child's actual age, the delayed child is unable to function at his true age level mentally. Lack of mental growth is life-debilitating.

Many Christians demonstrate physical and mental growth without signs of spiritual growth. They remain "babes in Christ." Lack of spiritual growth is life-limiting. The Lord wants us to develop in every aspect of life. We should continue to grow spiritually as well as physically and mentally.

Scripture teaches us that Jesus Christ grew in all areas of His life. Luke 2:52 says, "And Jesus grew in wisdom and stature, and in favor with God and men." The Son of God Himself demonstrated physical, mental, and spiritual growth. The Apostle Paul evidenced personal growth and encouraged growth in new believers. Paul wrote over half of the New Testament and honeycombed the Roman Empire with churches. In Philippians 3:13, he acknowledged his own need for growth. His epistles exhort Christians to grow in their faith and in their knowledge of their Savior.

Several of Paul's New Testament letters are addressed to individuals like Timothy and Titus who were beginning their own ministries. In 1 Timothy, Paul challenged his young friend to discipline himself personally and spiritually so that he could influence others. All of us should heed Paul's words of wisdom to Timothy:

> Discipline yourself for the purpose of godliness; for bodily discipline is only of little profit, but godliness is profitable for all things, since it holds promise for the present life and also for the life to come (1 Timothy 4:7,8 NAS).

We must practice self-control in every area of life as long as we live.

Christians should demonstrate growth in the disciplines of life — spiritual, personal, and mental. Failure to grow in even one area can cause dysfunction. We become out of balance when we cease growing in all areas simultaneously. The good news is that spiritual growth is not for spiritual giants only. All Christians can practice Spirit-controlled discipline to promote maturity and ensure obedience to Christ. It is the purpose of this chapter to identify specific areas of life where divine discipline can be exercised and to give practical suggestions for self-control.

Spiritual Discipline

Spiritual discipline is a result of submitting our self, our actions, and our desires to the authority of Jesus Christ. While discipline may seem painful and costly, it produces maturity. A Christian should not only accept Jesus as Savior but should also follow Him as Lord. We acknowledge His Lordship as we grow in Him daily and yield control of our lives to Him. This kind of devotion was evident in the lives of the men who followed Jesus during His ministry on earth.

The twelve disciples who ministered with Jesus demonstrated growth in all areas of their lives. They grew spiritually as they followed Jesus. The disciples listened to Jesus as He preached and taught. They learned from Jesus as He performed miracles and healed the sick. We, too, can experience spiritual growth as we spend time with Jesus. While we cannot minister with Him physically here on earth, we can minister in His power. Christians today can grow spiritually as they study the Word faithfully and pray continuously. As we mature spiritually, we begin to share the gospel with others and minister to their needs. Christ served others and commanded His disciples to serve in His name. All disciples of Jesus should go into the world making disciples of others (Matthew 28:19,20). However, if we are not disciplined spiritually, we will not go.

How can we grow spiritually? While it is not immediate or easy, persistence in daily devotion and service will produce spiritual growth. Let's talk specifically about three areas of spiritual discipline — Bible study, prayer, and witnessing. In chapter twelve we will discuss service to others. Growing Christians spend time with Jesus and serve Him faithfully.

Bible study is essential for spiritual growth. What food is to the physical life, God's Word is to spiritual life. The Bible reveals to us Who God is (John 5:39) and makes us aware of sin (Psalm 119:9-11). The Bible guides us and directs us throughout life (Proverbs 3:5,6). The Bible helps us live the life of a disciple (2 Timothy 3:16,17) and empowers us in our evangelism (Acts 22:14,15). If we fail to study God's Word for ourselves, we will not grow spiritually. Hebrews 5:12-14 says that we must learn the truths of God's Word so that we will mature. We will be considered mature when "by constant use (we) have trained (ourselves) to distinguish good from evil." Intensive, personal Bible study is necessary for spiritual growth.

Most of us sincerely believe that the Bible is God's inspired Word. However, we spend little time reading it or learning it. Active Christians often settle for hearing the Word in church and reading the Bible in Sunday School. We rarely pick up the Bible at home to study it for ourselves. The Navigators, a Christian organization, has a five-step plan for getting to know the Bible: (1) hear the Word, (2) read the Word, (3) study the Word, (4) memorize the Word, and (5) meditate on the Word. Each step requires daily discipline but promises spiritual growth. Here are some recommendations for learning the Bible in this way:

1. *Hear the Word* — listen regularly to the Bible preached from the pulpit, taught in your Sunday School class, and broadcast on radio or television.

2. *Read the Word* — get a schedule from your church for reading the Bible through each year or start by reading a chapter of Proverbs each day.

3. *Study the Word* — begin by studying your Sunday School lesson each week or follow a personal Bible study guide on a particular topic.

4. *Memorize the Word* — make a list of your favorite scriptures and start to memorize them one at a time.

5. *Meditate on the Word* — after reading or repeating a verse of Scripture, think about what it says to you and listen to God reveal His truth.

I pray that these suggestions will help you learn more of God's Word.

At times I am very faithful in my personal Bible study. Inevitably, though, my busy schedule squeezes out the time I set aside to study the Word. I barely manage to read the scriptures I must teach. When this happens, God convicts me of my need to be disciplined in Bible study. I start again to read a chapter of Proverbs each day or to study a specific book of the Bible. I also work on Scripture memorization. I like to write a special verse on an index card or "Post 'Em" sticker and place it in an obvious spot. Throughout the day, I read and reread the verse and memorize it word by word. What a blessing to have God's Word stored in my heart as a promise of assurance in times of need! Don't stop at memorizing the Word. Meditate on it, too! As we think about the Word, God reveals His truth to us.

Do you spend time daily studying the Bible? Are you disciplined in Scripture memory and faithful in your meditation? It's not too late to start or start again. The biggest mistake people make is thinking that a failure to be consistent is an excuse to give up. Ask God to give you the desire to know His Word and the perseverance to study it regularly. Make a plan for your personal Bible study. Most importantly, follow the plan daily so that you will demonstrate growth.

Spiritual discipline includes prayer as well as regular Bible study. The purpose of prayer is to converse with the Father (Jude 20,21). It is through prayer that we understand and know God (Jeremiah 9:23,24). We enjoy fellowship with God when we pray, and we receive guidance for our daily living. Although a sacrifice of time is necessary for us to commune with God through prayer, the strength and comfort prayer yields are well worth the effort. Growing Christians make prayer a priority in their lives.

If prayer has lost top priority in your life, then exercise divine discipline to resume your commitment. The following procedures may help you develop this spiritual discipline:

1. Set a definite time and a place for prayer.
2. Select some prayer resources (Bible, prayer journal, devotional book, etc.).
3. Form a prayer list to use daily or weekly. Revise it often.
4. Begin your prayer time with thanksgiving and praise.
5. Pray for yourself (personal requests) and on the behalf of others (petitions).
6. Conclude your prayer with confidence that God will answer. Your prayer life will improve if you take some definite action.

I have done two things recently which have dramatically improved my prayer life. First, I set aside a specific time and place to pray. Rather than waiting to see if I had time for God at the end of the day, I started to wake up fifteen minutes early so I could stop by a nearby coffeehouse for my prayer time on my way to work. That was a big commitment for me! (Remember, I'm not a morning person.) My time with the Lord is now a priority. Being out of my house protects me from many distractions. I made a prayer basket to take with me. It contains a prayer journal, a small Bible, a pen, a highlighter, and several notecards. I also included a flower from my prayer partner and a package of Kleenex for the tears I often shed. This prayer basket makes getting to my prayer time with everything I need very easy. A prayer basket has been a special and unique gift to many friends.

E. M. Bounds once said, "Our prayer chamber should have our freshest strength, our calmest time, its hours unfettered, without obtrusion, without haste. Private place and plenty of time are the life of prayer." All too often God gets our leftover time and energy. Rarely does He get our undivided attention for an unlimited time. I challenge you to set a time and a place for prayer. Be disciplined in your prayer life so that you will experience spiritual growth.

Christians must also be disciplined in witnessing. Witnessing should be the natural result of the spiritual growth which comes only through divine discipline. If God is at work in your life, you will want to witness. You will want to tell others of His power to save, restore, and direct lives. Why, then, are so many of us AWOL as witnesses? We seem paralyzed by fear — fear of inadequacy, of rejection, and of failure. Good news! God will help us overcome these fears: "For God did not give us a spirit of timidity, but a spirit of power, of love and of self-discipline" (2 Timothy 1:7). He gives us the ability, the concern, and the good judgment to be effective witnesses in our world.

A lifestyle example plus a verbal witness are essential tools for evangelism. *It is not enough to live a good life.* We must also be willing to speak a word about Jesus (1 Peter 3:15). There are many resources available to help us become better witnesses. Specific programs such as Continuing Witness Training and Evangelism Explosion provide intensive instruction for witnessing. Gospel tracts present a written plan of salvation. Marked Bibles can guide the Christian in sharing "the Roman road" or another Scripture plan. Whatever approach is most comfortable for you, there are resources available to help you. What God asks of us is a commitment to be a willing witness. A Christian must discipline herself to be a witness. Claim the power, love, and wisdom of God to overcome fear and become a bold witness.

Several years ago I asked my husband, who teaches evangelism at the New Orleans Baptist Theological Seminary, to help me become a better witness for the Lord. Chuck wrote a simple tract in the form of a thank-you note for me to use in sharing the gospel. That thank-you card includes a brief personal testimony as well as a simple plan of salvation. When I give the card to a waitress or clerk, I write a brief note of appreciation and sign my name plus the name of my church. The thank-you card often opens the door for a more direct witness. One waiter on receiving the thank-you card was sure that his mother, a faithful Christian praying for his salvation, had sent us to find him. We had a wonderful opportunity to talk with him about the Lord. Find some method that will help you become a more effective witness. You will experience spiritual growth as you share your faith.

One day at work I was the recipient of a feeble witnessing attempt. I stepped on the hospital elevator with only one other occupant. An elderly gentleman was standing nervously in the corner. Since I was on my way to see a new patient, I busied myself reading through the child's chart. The man exited the elevator before me and, as he did, he threw a piece of paper at me. As the doors closed, I reached down to pick up the paper. It was a gospel tract! Bless his heart. The man was scared to death of the doctor in the white coat. He didn't realize that the doctor was also a Christian who loved his Jesus, too. If the frightened man had spoken his word of witness, he would have learned of my faith and we could have rejoiced together. He taught me a very important lesson. He took the first step. He was determined to be a witness. His method may not have been ideal or polished, but he was faithful and obedient.

Are you willing to take the first step toward being a bold witness? Will you be faithful to share the gospel? Exercise the self-discipline necessary to be a witness for Jesus Christ to the people you meet each day. Commit today to a life of spiritual discipline through Bible study, prayer, fellowship, service, and witnessing.

Personal Discipline

The disciplines of life affect your spiritual condition and your personal life. A Christian with self-control shows spiritual maturity as well as personal growth. *Daily discipline is necessary for self-improvement and personal achievement.* Every individual must learn to control his body, his reputation, and his purpose in order to maintain personal discipline.

Our society seems more interested in health and fitness today than ever before. Fitness is in! Even fast-food restaurants offer healthy foods today. A wide range of aerobic exercises are offered to strengthen the heart and tone the muscles. But, we still have a problem with self-control. We just can't stick to a diet or exercise program. Does that sound familiar? Let's think about physical discipline.

Nutrition and fitness are important for many obvious reasons. For the Christian, they are an act of obedience to Christ. While outward beauty should not be the primary goal, good nutrition and regular exercise improve overall health and increase vitality. A Christian who eats healthy foods and remains physically active is better conditioned for service and better prepared to witness. We cannot become the people God would have us be if we are not fit for the Kingdom.

There are numerous scriptural teachings about physical discipline. Psalm 139:13-18 informs us that our bodies are gifts from God. God not only created us, but He still owns us. Thus, we are only the caretakers of our bodies which are possessions of God. New Testament scriptures tell us of our responsibilities to give our bodies back to God (Romans 12:1) and take care of our bodies (1 Corinthians 6:19,20). Disciplined believers should dedicate their bodies to God and tend to their bodies for Him. It is such a blessing to realize that God created each of us specially and gave each one of us a specific purpose. It is our duty to take care of our bodies so that we can serve Him without hindrance.

In order to develop healthy eating habits, you must avoid unhealthy foods and eat nutritious ones. If you don't know much about nutrition, buy some books or read some magazine articles to educate yourself. Try to limit foods with high fat and high sodium content. Begin to analyze the labels on the products you buy in order to make wise selections. Increase your consumption of fruits, vegetables, and grains. Use cooking methods that limit fat: grilling, baking, broiling, and steaming. Control the amount of food you eat. Prepare smaller portions. Put some food aside for another meal. Don't be afraid to throw food away. Don't feel obligated to eat everything on the table.

The following nutrition tips have been helpful to me in controlling my eating:

1. *Remember that you can control what you eat.* Avoid tempting foods until you can eat them in moderation.

2. *Don't let anyone love you with food.* Discourage gifts of food. Do not reward yourself with food.

3. *Eat smaller amounts, more often.* Small, frequent, healthy meals are advised since eating often keeps the metabolism burning calories at a higher level. Don't skip meals.

4. *Learn about foods and a balanced diet.* Plan your menus to guarantee healthful eating and decrease binge eating.

5. *Throw food away or save it for later.* Measure your portions, then stop eating. A small, full plate looks more satisfying than a large, half-empty plate.

6. *Choose an eating place. When eating, only eat.* Focus on eating and eat slowly so that you will truly enjoy your meal.

7. *Avoid high-sodium, high-cholesterol foods.* Reduce your intake of refined sugar, fat, and salt. These substances have been related to various health problems.

8. *Consider the nutritional content, not just the calories.* All calories are not created equal. Concentrate instead on limiting fat to 30 percent of total calories daily (three grams of fat per 100 calories).

9. *Measure success by fit of clothes, not loss of pounds.* Exercise may develop muscles that weigh more than fat. Toned muscles make clothes fit better (and look better!).

10. *Remember that healthful eating is the goal, not dieting.* Eliminate the word "diet" from your vocabulary. Learn healthy eating that will last a lifetime.

If you want to stay disciplined in your fitness, you must find the best type of exercise for you. You need not follow the jogging trend or walk with a friend if you don't like it. There is a form of exercise to please everyone. Generally speaking, there are five basic aerobic exercises: walking, running/jogging, swimming, cycling, and aerobic dance. Choose the activity you find most enjoyable, relaxing, and convenient and get started. Stick to your fitness regime and you will be successful.

I have compiled a list of ten fitness tips that can help you begin regular exercise and maintain physical discipline:

1. *There is not one best way to exercise.* Find the right type of exercise for you. The wrong exercise for you is a sure path to failure.

2. *Vary your type of exercise.* Select two or three different exercise routines and change them with the seasons or your moods.

3. *Exercise for your health, not your figure.* The primary goal of exercise should be good health. Toning flabby muscles and reducing inches will be side benefits.

4. *Sustained exercise for twenty to thirty minutes three times a week is a reasonable goal.* The cardiovascular system needs at least twenty to thirty minutes of ongoing exercise to get a good workout. Start with shorter periods and build up.

5. *Warm up before exercise, then cool down after exercise.* Begin with stretching and mobility exercises to prevent injuries. A slow

start and easy finish also helps you adjust mentally for exercise.

6. *Make exercise fun and convenient.* Find inventive ways to make exercise fun. Try to weave your exercise permanently into your busy schedule.

7. *Seek peer support or an exercise partner.* Peer pressure and camaraderie encourage continued fitness. Join an exercise group or find a committed partner.

8. *Set realistic goals, then reward your accomplishments.* Decide on a desired type and reasonable amount of exercise for your lifestyle. Give yourself nonfood rewards when you accomplish your individual goals.

9. *Start!* Don't wait until you have the time or until the conditions are perfect to begin your exercise program. There will never be extra minutes in the day and the factors will never be just right. So, don't delay!

10. *Keep it up!* Make a daily recommitment to exercise. Remember that lapses happen to all of us. Start again whether it's for the second time or the twentieth.

Do you remember the decision that Marjorie Holmes related in her book, *Secrets of Health, Energy, and Staying Young*? In a previous chapter, I told you that she chose to stay fit. As a young child, Mrs. Holmes recognized that her mother's family was lean and her father's family was fat. She deliberately decided to stay lean like her mother's family. Have you ever made a deliberate decision to take care of your body? It is never too late for that commitment. Each of us can choose to stay healthy and fit. Daily recommitment to healthy eating and regular exercise will help us develop personal discipline.

Christians also must be disciplined in personal purity. The starkest contrast between nonbelievers and believers in this world should be their lifestyles. The reputations of Christians are at great risk today. It is obvious that Satan is alive and at work in the world. The evil one is busy attacking the unbeliever and the believer alike. He wants to keep the lost under his control and he wants to bring the saved under his power. Be on guard, Christian! You are under personal attack. The devil is after your loved ones, too. Ephesians 6 warns us: "Put on the full armor of God so that you can take your stand against the devil's schemes" (verse 11). Christians must wear God's armor to protect their personal purity and ensure victory in spiritual warfare.

The greatest enemies of the Christian are pride, money, and lust. When we believe that we are sufficient, the result is exalted self-worth. When we focus on financial gain, the result is decreased trust in God's faithful provision. When we think evil thoughts, the result is flagrant sin. If we Christians are aware of our human weaknesses, we will become better able to resist the temptation of the devil. James 1:15 says, "After desire has conceived, it gives birth to sin; and sin, when it is full-grown, gives birth to death." We must try to control our sinful natures and remain pure in our spirits, our bodies, our thoughts, our speech, our business dealings, and our personal relationships.

Unfortunately, Satan has defeated many believers in their personal purity. A low standard of Christian living is not new in our generation. We have been fighting the battle against sin for ages. Though Hannah Whitall Smith wrote this statement in the late 1800s in her book, *The Christian's Secret of a Happy Life*, it accurately reflects society today:

> The standard of practical holy living has been so low among Christians that very often the person who tries to practice spiritual disciplines in everyday life is looked upon with disapproval by a large portion of the Church. And for the most part, the followers of Jesus Christ are satisfied with a life so conformed to the world, and so like it in almost every respect, that to a casual observer, there is no difference between the Christian and the pagan (page 130).

We must not settle for conformity to the world. We must strive for personal purity. While godly living is not easy, the Holy Spirit empowers us as we persist in divine discipline.

Finally, Christians must be disciplined in their life's purpose. If we desire personal growth as well as spiritual maturity, we must determine God's plan for our lives and then establish lifelong goals and daily priorities to fulfill His plan. A disciplined believer should order specific priorities around Jesus (Philippians 3:13,14). Visualize a wheel with Christ as the hub or center. Your life priorities represent the spokes of the wheel. The wheel will stay in balance as long as the hub (Jesus Christ) remains consistently in the center.

When our priorities get out of balance and when Jesus is no longer central to our lives, the wheel cannot roll. *Many Christians lose control of their lives because Jesus is not the focus.* A challenge of personal discipline is to focus on Jesus and clarify our purpose as we keep our priorities in balance.

I am often frustrated by what seems to be a lack of time. In my study of time management strategies, however, I have learned that we have all the time we need and we all have the same amount of time. Those facts don't add any hours to the day, but they do help me learn to use my time more wisely and efficiently. These twelve timely tips have taught me to be more productive. I hope they will help you, too.

1. You have all the time you need.
2. Plan your time or others will do it for you.
3. Leave a margin for the unexpected.
4. Do one thing at a time and finish it.
5. Learn to say no.
6. Separate the important from the urgent.
7. Use shortcuts to promote efficiency.
8. Be decisive. Make up your mind as quickly as possible.
9. Write it down so you won't forget it.
10. Be time conscious.
11. Work smarter not harder.
12. Set your course and stick to it.

Efficient control of time is critical to personal discipline.

Jesus' twelve disciples grew spiritually, but they also grew personally. That is the challenge for all of us who want to be faithful disciples. God adds His supernatural power and people provide their persuasive power to supplement our limited willpower in this process called divine discipline. God's Word records the spiritual and personal maturity of the disciples as well as their mental growth. These disciplines of life are to be the pursuit of all Christians.

Mental Discipline

If Jesus increased in wisdom and knowledge and if He is to be our model for living, then we Christians should grow in our judgment and understanding. Like spiritual maturity and personal development, mental growth requires self-discipline and perseverance. These disciplines of life are a part of our growing faith.

Wisdom is the power to judge rightly and follow the sound course of action. It is an acquisition based on experience more than training. Wisdom is often a virtue used to describe the elderly. Years of experience in life provide a foundation of wisdom. Few people in our society today live near their families. We have become separated geographically. As a result, children rarely see their grandparents. We miss out on the wisdom of our older relatives. However, we can learn from older Christians in our churches. Elderly Christians have so much wisdom to share with younger believers. We must seek their wise counsel and copy their mental discipline.

In the Old Testament, leaders and prophets sought wisdom from God. The psalmist David pled for godly wisdom in Psalm 51, a song of forgiveness and restoration. He depended on true wisdom to make important decisions and live a righteous life. Isaiah prophesied of the Messiah's infinite wisdom when he said:

> The Spirit of the Lord will rest on him —
> the Spirit of wisdom and of understanding,
> the Spirit of counsel and of power,
> the Spirit of knowledge and of the fear of the Lord
> (Isaiah 11:2).

Even Solomon in the Proverbs wrote about the wealth of wisdom. In Proverbs 1, he challenged the righteous to allow wisdom to govern their lives. Specifically, his precepts of wisdom warned the godly to avoid bad company (verses 8-19) and heed wise counsel (verses 20-33). The value of wisdom is echoed in the New Testament.

The Pauline epistles include frequent exhortation for believers to seek wisdom from God. In Ephesians 1:17, Paul records his prayer to fellow Christians in Ephesus. He prays earnestly that "the God of our Lord Jesus Christ, the glorious Father, may give you the Spirit of wisdom and revelation." True wisdom is a gift of God. Paul listed wisdom in his description of spiritual gifts in 1 Corinthians 12:4-11.

The ability to communicate wisdom, along with other spiritual gifts, is for ministry and service to others not for personal edification.

Although only some gifted believers possess extraordinary wisdom, all disciplined believers are to seek spiritual wisdom. James 1:5 reminds us that wisdom is available to all who ask in faith: "If any of you lacks wisdom, he should ask God, who gives generously to all without finding fault, and it will be given to him."

I constantly seek spiritual wisdom and sound judgment from the Lord. He is always faithful when I ask with confidence. I have learned that God really does give wisdom for real-life decisions. One of my toughest decisions was faced recently. Chuck and I began to pray about my work schedule. Just as opportunities for ministry were emerging, the demands of the office were increasing. A time crunch! As we prayed for wisdom concerning my work schedule, God began to pull the pieces together. A new speech therapist joined my staff, allowing me to reduce my caseload. A newly appointed assistant director began to share some of my administrative responsibilities. I was able to take a leave of absence in order to accompany Chuck overseas for a six-week sabbatical. When we returned, the decision was clear. God had put everything in place for me to reduce my schedule by ten hours per week. While we asked in faith believing, God was at work answering our prayers for wisdom. We should praise God for the guidance He gives us.

I am also grateful for the loving counsel of older Christian friends. I listen carefully to the suggestions of those who are wise. A special godly lady in our church has become a treasured friend and loving advisor. This ninety-two-year-old saint made a suggestion that has tremendously improved our monthly prayer group. She loaned me a book on conversational prayer by Rosalind Rinker suggesting that we spend more time in prayer than in talking about prayer requests. After reading *Prayer: Conversing with God*, I agreed that our requests and petitions could be expressed to each other as we talked to God. We now use all our time together for prayer. Many have benefitted from Mrs. Seaman's participation in other prayer groups through the years. I thank the Lord for the wisdom of His children.

Proverbs 4:5 exhorts the reader to acquire wisdom and knowledge. Knowledge is the accumulation of information and learning. In contrast to the experience of wisdom, knowledge encompasses understanding and awareness that must be taught. While wisdom is experienced, knowledge is learned. Both are characteristics of Jesus Christ and His followers.

At times I feel very knowledgeable. After all, I do have twenty-five years of education! Between us, my husband and I have been in school more than fifty years. We're not professional students, just pursuers of higher education. But Chuck and I have learned that books don't teach you everything. Information read in books may help you carry on a good conversation, but many important things are learned only through experiences. I often feel that I have extensive specialized learning but only limited practical experience.

Shortly after we completed our doctorates, Chuck and I moved into a house on the seminary campus. One day we realized that the grass needed to be cut. Who would be responsible for cutting the grass? Neither of us had ever mowed a lawn. We decided to do it together. We both tried to start the lawn mower we had been given. I read the manual aloud while Chuck tried to start it. After forty-five minutes, we still did not have the lawn mower started. We began to laugh hysterically when we realized that despite all our knowledge, we couldn't mow our grass. We had no experience. Both knowledge and wisdom are essential for mental growth.

God wants us to increase in knowledge — His divine understanding. The knowledge of God is wonderful and difficult to attain (Psalm 139:6). However, wise men store up God's knowledge while fools remain satisfied with their own (Proverbs 10:14). Knowledge is a godly virtue that helps God's children control their tongues and their tempers (Proverbs 17:27). Though knowledge should be sought after, the love of Christ "surpasses knowledge" (Ephesians 3:19). If we are truly smart, we will express our love for Jesus more than we seek to understand His truths.

The prophet Isaiah foretold the birth of the Messiah. He also prophesied about the second coming of Jesus. During the future reign of the Son of God, the world will be filled with harmony. Isaiah said that only then will the earth be full of the knowledge of the Lord (Isaiah 11:9). Until that time, God's children are to pursue spiritual knowledge for themselves and proclaim His wisdom to others. The pursuit of knowledge is a worthwhile endeavor for a Christian. We are to "grow in the grace and knowledge of our Lord and Savior Jesus Christ" (2 Peter 3:18). That kind of knowledge requires spiritual growth, personal development, and mental discipline.

The commitment to increase in wisdom and knowledge must

continue throughout life. The resulting spiritual wisdom and lasting knowledge are eternal rewards of divine discipline. In Romans 11:33, Paul rejoiced in "the depth of the riches both of the wisdom and knowledge of God." While God's judgments and His precepts are hard to comprehend, they are easy to claim by all who ask in faith.

Some days I feel that the most significant information I read is the Cathy cartoon. Her humor always brightens my day. Though she is great for comic relief, I can't depend on Cathy Guisewite for all of my wisdom and knowledge. God wants to teach me through my personal experience and intensive study. If I discipline myself daily, I will increase in wisdom and knowledge like Jesus. One of my primary goals for mental growth this year is to read one significant book every month. I can't count novels or fiction. Already I have learned a lot through this mental discipline.

The original disciples provide models of growth and maturity for us today. Those followers of Christ disciplined themselves in their daily lives in order to experience the spiritual maturity, personal development, and mental growth necessary to serve their Lord. As contemporary Christians, we, too, should develop and maintain self-control. If the disciples who ministered with Jesus Christ grew spiritually, personally, and mentally, shouldn't we? If we profess Christ as Savior and serve Him as Lord, we must practice divine discipline until He returns.

BIBLICAL STUDY

Carefully read the following scripture: 1 Corinthians 9:24-27. Answer these questions about the disciplines of life.

1. Who runs the race? _____

2. Who wins the race? _____

3. Who receives the rewards? _____

PERSONAL APPLICATION

1. Are you disciplined in your spiritual life? List below several specific goals for your spiritual growth.

2. Are you disciplined in your personal life? In the space below, write at least three goals for personal development.

3. Are you disciplined in your mental life? Ask God to help you increase in wisdom and knowledge. Write your plan for mental discipline below.

Dear Lord,

Thank You for Your strength and guidance in the search for divine discipline. Help me develop and maintain spiritual maturity, personal development, and mental growth. Then I will ready to share the message of self-discipline with others.

Amen

CHAPTER 12

Divine Discipline Can Change the World
(Self-Control and Others)

> Train the younger women to love their husbands and children, to be self-controlled and pure, to be busy at home, to be kind, and to be subject to their husbands, so that no one will malign the word of God (Titus 2:4,5).

All of us would agree we live in an undisciplined world. The people around us and we ourselves lack discipline in many areas of life. Much of the crime, illness, and apathy in our society is the result of poor self-control. A recent survey reported that 51 percent of the Americans sampled were not physically fit because they admitted that they had no self-discipline. Our generation is aptly described as "couch potatoes" or "armchair quarterbacks." Many have forgotten the importance of discipline in daily living.

Self-discipline is necessary in all aspects of life. However, we often invest our time and energy in less important activities, neglecting the truly important matters of life. Gordon Dahl once said, "Most middle-class Americans tend to worship their work, to work at their play, and to play at their worship. As a result, their meanings and values are distorted. Their relationships disintegrate faster than they can keep them in repair, and their lifestyles resemble a cast of characters in search of a plot." Does this sound like you or people you know? We need to be disciplined in the most important matters of life.

While difficulty with self-control is universal, some people develop significant disorders of self-control. In his book, *Counseling for Problems of Self-Control*, psychologist R. P. Walters discusses specific disorders of self-control including compulsive drinking, overeating, shoplifting, gambling, and smoking. He also considers the excesses of gossip, violent anger, and pornography. Certainly these are obvious examples of extreme loss of self-control. While we are distressed by the impact of these abuses on other people, we also see the reality of their disruption in our own lives. Disorders of self-control cause personal pain within and fractured harmony without. Dr. Walters says that disorders of self-control are "ugly, discordant conditions, with as many variations as notes on a piano, including the cracks" (page 11). As growing Christians, we must develop self-control in our own lives and teach others to pursue divine discipline.

Humanists say that we should be able to obtain self-control in our own strength. I have tried repeatedly, and I have failed every time. It is impossible for any individual to maintain self-control in his own power. Human effort is limited and superficial. We may achieve momentary control, but in time we return to our insufficient, sinful ways. However, as believers we can claim the supernatural power of God to maintain divine discipline. *The key to gaining self-control is yielding control of the self to the control of the Holy Spirit.* Self-control is possible! Scriptures call for it, the Holy Spirit enables it, disciplined Christians pursue it, and obedient followers teach it. We can promote divine discipline in others as we build them up, lift them up, and train them up.

Build Them Up!

The Bible clearly teaches Christians that we are to encourage one another. In the same way that the affirmation of others helps us develop divine discipline, our encouragement can build self-control in others. Although we cannot produce self-control in others, we can influence them with our Spirit-empowered self-control. My journey toward self-discipline began with my sincere desire to change myself. Over the months as I have had the opportunity to share this message, God has used me to challenge others. It is my prayer that all Christians will learn the power of divine discipline and, then, share what they have learned with our lost and hopeless world. Minister to the people — build them up!

One of the strongest themes of Ephesians is a challenge for godly living. In chapter 4, Paul gives specific instructions for our relationships with others. After salvation, we are to have new life in Christ. New life results in new behavior. Believers are to speak the truth at all times (Ephesians 4:25) and not remain angry with others (verse 26).

We are not to steal; we are to earn a living to provide for our own needs and to enable us to assist others (verse 28). Paul summarizes the characteristics of the new life in Ephesians 4:29:

> Do not let any unwholesome talk come out of your mouths, but only what is helpful for building others up according to their needs, that it may benefit those who listen.

If we want to change the world, we must use divine discipline to build each other up. Our human natures are much more content to tear each other down. Critical words and bitter comments flow easily from our mouths. Our harsh, painful words can destroy a person's spirit. It takes a lot of affirmation and kindness to build that individual back. Criticism is natural to us, but God gives us the power to control our tongues and to speak words that will encourage others. *Our words can benefit and bless rather than hurt and harm.*

Do you enjoy the beach? I do. (My sweet husband simply tolerates it with me.) Time in the sun and surf is so relaxing to me. I usually try to read while sunbathing, but I often become distracted by my people-watching. I love to watch everyone, but I especially like to watch children build castles in the sand. Many times a child will begin to construct a sandcastle too close to the ocean. Before long, the waves roll in and knock the castle down. After all, that is what waves do. Our lives are filled with words that tear us down like waves tear down sandcastles. We need the consistent encouragement of Christians to build us up while the sinfulness of the world tries to tear us down. God wants us to be wise and persistent as we edify each other.

In their book, *When You Feel Like Screaming,* Pat Holt and Dr. Grace Ketterman include the results of a questionnaire. They asked 150 children between nine and twelve years of age this question: "What do you dislike most about your mother?" Almost every child answered, "Her screaming." A mother's uncontrolled anger is a destructive tool that tears down her children. Mothers know that screaming upsets their children, but the screaming habit is hard to break. One of the greatest challenges for mothers is to build up their children with positive, affirming words while the world tries constantly to tear them down. Remember that calm, controlled mothers breed calm, controlled children. Ask God to give you a loving spirit and kind words as you face the daily demands of parenting.

This old inscription contains great wisdom for mothers who want to build up their children. While we are uncertain of the author, the truth of the words is certain:

> That woman who is cool and collected,
> who is master of her countenance,
> her voice, her actions, and her gestures,
> will be the mother who is in control of her children,
> and who is greatly beloved by them.

Those words will describe us all if we use divine discipline to build each other up.

This world can be changed as we practice divine discipline. The Holy Spirit will help us understand others so that we can affirm them. God didn't make us all alike. Aren't you glad? We must learn to *understand* and accept differences in people. Different is not bad, it is just different. We can build others up when we understand them. We will understand them better as we listen to them speak and observe their actions. Disciplined Christians will also *acknowledge* the good in others. Praise for deeds well done is always better than criticism for shortcomings. I'm a firm believer in positive reinforcement! Finally, we must learn to *strengthen* each other. Our love and concern will give additional strength to the power God gives His children. Where there is hatred, let us sow love. If love forms the foundation, then kind words build up the walls. Be on God's construction crew in the world, not the devil's demolition derby.

How can you build up others? Begin by eliminating negative, critical words from your vocabulary. Replace them with positive, loving words. "Bad" and "stupid" should be changed to "good" and "smart." Try to find the good in everyone. Sometimes you may have to look deeply, but everyone has a strength. Start every day with glory to the Lord and praise for others. My dad used to say, "Most people wake up saying, 'Good Lord, it's morning!' instead of, 'Good morning, Lord.'" Begin your day with praise. When you hear yourself say harsh or unkind words, stop immediately. Ask God to change your heart, then He can change your words. Take joy in saying nice things to others. As you recall the kindness of a friend, tell her of your appreciation or write a note of thanks. A spoken or written word of encouragement takes some effort on your part, but it does a lot to build up another person.

Florence Littauer agrees that there is great power in a word. In her book, *Silver Boxes*, Mrs. Littauer shares biblical principles about encouragement that she taught her own children. Based on Ephesians 4:29, the book supports the belief that words need to build people up. She says, "Our words should be gifts to each other, little silver boxes with bows on top" (page 4). Her book is filled with wit and wisdom for encouragers. It is a "how to" book that suggests creative ways to edify one another in the name of the Lord. Remember that your words make a difference to others.

The following list of do's and don'ts was compiled from a study of Ephesians 4:17-32. It summarizes the positive attributes we would wish to increase and the negative attributes we would wish to eliminate:

DO'S	DON'TS
(Christians should be ...)	(Christians should not be ...)
understanding	ignorant
tenderhearted	hardhearted
sensitive	callous
pure	impure
generous	greedy
righteous	corrupt
truthful	deceitful
angry	bitter
honest	dishonest
supportive	destructive
forgiving	vengeful
encouraging	discouraging

If we allow the Holy Spirit to help us, we can build each other up with love.

Lift Them Up!

Divine discipline is necessary to give encouragement to others. It also takes supernatural self-control to minister to those in need. If we Christians want to change our world for Christ, we cannot be satisfied with the personal benefits of self-discipline. We must be willing to share the benefits of self-discipline with others. We give our self-control to others when we build them up and lift them up. Divine discipline can change the world.

In 2 Corinthians 1:4, Paul says that God "comforts us in all our troubles, so that we can comfort those in any trouble with the comfort we ourselves have received from God." God comforts us so we can comfort others. *God lifts us up so we can lift up others.* We must discipline ourselves to meet the needs of others, to minister to the lost and lonely, to lift up the down and out. God will give us the power to minister in His name.

There are so many needy people in our world. Some people need salvation, while others need the joy of their salvation. Some need food, while others eat too much. Some need clothes, while others buy too many. Some need shelter, while others have excessively large homes. No matter what the need, Jesus can provide. No matter what the problem, Jesus is the answer. Disciplined Christians must be available instruments for God to use in meeting the needs of others. Reaching out in love takes time and commitment, but it will lift people up.

Several years ago, Denise came into our lives. She came to church one Sunday morning, obviously burdened by her problems. At twenty-one years of age, she had already experienced more in life than I could imagine. She came from a broken home and was already divorced herself. She was raised by a single mother who was now raising Denise's own son. She had been addicted to drugs and tried rehabilitation. She had been sexually abused and physically neglected. What needs! When confronted with her problems, I felt overwhelmed and helpless. But, the Holy Spirit began to use me to lift her up.

Denise came to live with us for several months and started to work at our church preschool center. We led her to the Lord and helped her grow in her faith. We tried to meet her physical and spiritual needs. While her problems didn't go away, she demonstrated growth and maturity. Denise decided to attend a college outside the New Orleans area. In time we lost contact with her. Our letters to her were returned unopened. Her overdue bills were forwarded to our home. We could not find her. Though we worried about her safety and her spiritual condition, all we could do was pray for her. Just recently, Denise called. She has remarried and has another son. Her husband is a Christian. Together they are active in a church in Florida. We are so grateful that we were obedient in meeting her spiritual and physical needs. Her life is changed because we allowed God to use us to minister to her.

Albert Schweitzer once said, "The purpose of life is to serve and to show compassion and the will to help others. Only then have we ourselves become true human beings." If you want to be a true human being, help others. If you want to grow as a Christian, reach out to others. Ministry to others is both giving and receiving. As we serve others, we ourselves are served. There is great joy in our service. As we love others, we, too, are loved. God's love is poured out on us for our obedience.

People all around us have needs. There are needs within our community. There are hurts among the family of God as well as among our friends in the world. We are called to be sensitive to the needs of others and willing to minister as needed. Within the church, the body of believers, there are emotional, physical, intellectual, and spiritual needs. While we Christians enjoy fellowship with one another, we don't always minister to one another effectively. After-church fellowships are fun, but they don't heal the deep hurts of many believers. Church members need to practice biblical fellowship which provides encouragement and promotes spiritual growth. Hebrews 10:24,25 calls us to "consider how we may spur one another on toward love and good deeds. Let us not give up meeting together, as some are in the habit of doing, but let us encourage one another — and all the more as you see the Day approaching."

Women's ministries within the local church are growing. Women are open to discuss their own problems and they are ready to help others with their problems. Look right around you on Sunday morning or Wednesday night and you will see many women within the church with serious needs. Some of these suggestions may help you reach those in your church who are hurting:

1. Find someone with a problem like yours and begin to work on it together.
2. Start a prayer group or prayer chain to pray specifically for those in need within your fellowship.
3. Find one woman with a special need and disciple her, minister to her directly.
4. Ask a new Christian to be your Bible study partner, meet regularly to study the scriptures and discuss their meaning.
5. Form small special interest groups to discuss common problems and biblical solutions.
6. Open your home to those in need for hospitality and fellowship.

Discipling One Another was written by Anne Ortlund and offers suggestions for discipleship of other Christians. It includes recommendations for meeting the physical, mental, and spiritual needs of others. In addition, Linda R. McGinn has written a helpful book entitled *Resource Guide for Women's Ministries*. It is filled with ideas for ministry to both Christian women and unsaved ladies. We need to care for one another within the fellowship of God and we need to reach out to others with salvation.

The Great Commission to Christians was given by our Lord in Matthew 28:19,20. Jesus said:

> "Go and make disciples of all nations, baptizing them in the name of the Father and of the Son and of the Holy Spirit, and teaching them to obey everything I have commanded you. And surely I am with you always, to the very end of the age."

A mature follower of Christ will meet the spiritual needs of others by sharing a personal witness. Are you lifting people up through the saving power of Jesus Christ? If not, discipline yourself to witness to others. If so, continue faithfully your work for the Lord.

Christians can lift up the lost by meeting needs in the name of Jesus. A good deed done without a word of witness will seem like simple kindness. However, ministry to needs with a strong verbal witness will bring others to Jesus. These suggestions may help you lift up the lost:

1. Communicate the gospel clearly in everyday interactions. Give God praise for blessings in your life.

2. Tell unsaved friends that you are praying for them. Don't say "good luck" but "God bless."

3. Have lost friends in your home often. Prayer before meals and family devotionals can be a witness.

4. Welcome new neighbors with a basket of goodies plus a gospel tract and brochure about your church.

5. Plan special events in your home or church and invite lost friends to come.

   Be sure to give God the glory so that you can lead others to Him.

Disciplined believers will serve others. Jesus, our perfect example, served others; so should we. Service is doing something to meet the needs of someone else. The local church is the best context for service. Many programs within the church offer opportunities for ministry to others in the name of Jesus. Evidence of a servant's heart includes a willingness to do even menial tasks, an availability to others at all times, an awareness of the needs of others, and a desire to do more than is required. Do you have a servant's heart? Your servant's heart will help lift people up.

During high school, I had a special friend named Vanee. She was the only child of older parents who rarely attended church. She began to visit my house and my church. She seemed to enjoy my loving home with its Christian atmosphere. One summer I invited her to go to Youth Camp with me. She had a great time. She came home truly changed. I had the joy of leading her to the Lord as we talked on the swing late one night. I am grateful that God used me to lift her up. Vanee has continued to grow in her faith and is now serving the Lord as a missionary in Wyoming. She has learned to encourage and train others.

God wants all of His children to be encouragers and helpers. He needs us to comfort others in His name. He will supply our needs so that we can reach out to others. There are many ways for us to change the world, but first we must be committed to the task and make the time regularly for ministry. The Lord wants us to be builders and helpers. He also wants us to be teachers.

Train Them Up!

Why must we teach others to be encouragers? Why must we train others to be self-disciplined? All of us need to learn to be more dedicated as encouragers and more committed to discipline. Because we may feel incapable or inadequate to live a godly life on our own, we need the instruction of mature Christians. When we trust Jesus as Savior, we want to share Him with others. When we start controlling ourselves, we can begin to teach control to others.

Titus 2 is a common theme for women in ministry. It gives older Christians the specific responsibility of teaching younger Christians about godly living. Paul challenged Titus to teach his young converts sound doctrines that would cause them to behave as they believed. In Titus 2:4,5, older women were told to:

> Train the younger women to love their husbands and children,
> and be self-controlled and pure, to be busy at home, to be kind,
> and to be subject to their husbands, so that no one will malign
> the word of God.

By word and deed, mature believers teach the young to be loving, pure, productive, kind, submissive, and self-controlled. The young in faith will not grow unless we discipline ourselves to train them.

A group of ladies in a Florida church has established a community ministry to teach the younger women. They call themselves the "Titus 2 Women." These ladies not only meet personal needs, but they train others to help them reach out. They provide food for newcomers, help new homeowners decorate, and sew for the needy. The older ladies help the young mothers with child-care and carpools. While meeting real-life needs, they also give spiritual food. As the young women become strong, they are encouraged to join the group in ministry to others. What a creative way, a truly biblical way, to build others up, lift them up, and train them up.

Proverbs 22:6 is not only a challenge for parents, but a promise as well. Parents are to "train a child in the way he should go, and when he is old he will not turn from it." Parenting is an awesome responsibility demanding daily self-control. We can be confident that if we teach our children the important things of God they will not forsake His teachings. Though our children may turn away from the Lord and their parents for a time, what an assurance to know that our training will not leave them. As parents we need to discipline, but also to encourage self-discipline. Our children must learn to be control themselves. Only then will they become the mature, happy Christians that God desires for them to be and that we want them to be. It is a parent's responsibility to train her children in divine discipline.

My mother told me of an experience during a recent visit with my sister and her family. One of my nephews was in a bad mood and was making it obvious to everyone. When my mother corrected him, he quickly lashed out and said, "You're too mean to be a grandmother." Immediately his mother took him to his room to discipline him. They emerged later and he apologized to his grandmother for his lack of respect. My sister's task as a mother was not only to discipline her child's misbehavior but also to encourage him to control his own behavior. Parents must train their children to be self-controlled.

Emilie Barnes discusses ways to train others in her book, *Things Happen When Women Care*. She believes that hospitality and friendship are desperately needed in today's busy world. We must make the time to reach out to others. Parents must teach their children to make time to meet needs. She wrote: "If our family is to survive, we must find time and opportunities to train our children to have skills that make them have a meaningful attitude toward being a member of our family" (page 65). Parents need to teach their children to care about others instead of being consumed by their own needs.

I am grateful that I am active in a very missions-minded church. Our church supports mission work not only in the world and the nation, but in our community as well. There are many social and spiritual needs in New Orleans. We encourage our members to give to missions and to pray for missions, but we also challenge them to become involved in missions. Families make the time to take food to a housing project together or to spend an evening talking with foreign travelers at the Seaman's Center. Parents should not protect their children from the problems of the world. Rather, they should teach them to minister to those needs.

Recently I invited a local missionary to speak to the group of young girls I work with each Wednesday night. Since we are a mission group, we always pray for missionaries and give money for missions. Many of the girls, however, were unaware of the serious needs in their own community. As the missionary showed slides of her work, the girls were significantly affected by a picture of a homeless man sleeping on a bench. Many of them could not imagine anyone not having a home. They bombarded the missionary with questions. Several of them wanted to take the man home with them. Others wanted the church to shelter him. They became burdened by the problems in our own city. Months later they are still praying by name for the homeless man. We must teach our young to care for the needs of others and to take time to minister in Jesus' name.

Marsha Spradlin's book, *Women of Faith in the 90's*, reminds us of our responsibility to make a difference in the world. She tells the stories of women in crisis — neighbors, friends, or co-workers. As obedient Christians, we must minister in love. As disciplined believers, we must train others to minister. *Have the courage to care and the discipline to disciple.* You can make a difference as you touch lives in love. Marsha Spradlin concludes that "virtually every aspect of the human experience has been enormously affected by those who give their time, their love, and their life unselfishly to others" (page 120). Our divine discipline can change the world!

Now that you have learned about divine discipline, it is your responsibility to teach it to others. As God changes your life, He will change others through you. Your world may include a spouse, children, family, friends, neighbors, or customers. Each of them needs to see your example of self-control and hear your message of divine discipline. With the help of the Lord, you can share the gospel message and meet real-life needs. Persevere as you encourage and teach others. Many of them will be slow learners — slow to understand the things of God. But if you continue to lift them up and train them in godly living, others will be encouraged by your love and may become involved in ministry with you. Nothing is more thrilling than to see spiritual growth in a young Christian you disciple. There are great rewards in training others to be self-controlled.

Ann Kiemel Anderson closed her book, *I'm Out to Change My World*, with this prayer:

> May we cry with them as you cry with us,
> and laugh with them as you laugh with us;
> and may they know you by your love in us,
> and that you and I and our brothers in love
> can change the world (page 119).

Let that be our prayer as we, through divine discipline, seek to change the world.

BIBLICAL STUDY

Carefully read Titus 2:2-8. It may help you to read it in several different Bible translations. Complete the sentences below about ways in which we as Christians can change the world.

Older men should be _____

_____.

Older men should teach younger men to be _____

_____.

Older women should be _____

_____.

Older women should teach younger women to be _____

_____.

PERSONAL APPLICATION

1. Think about some words of encouragement that you have spoken recently. Have you said something that would lift someone up? Write your encouraging words in the space below and remember the blessing you received from giving encouragement.

Try to build others up — give at least five compliments a day.

2. Have you involved your family in ministering to the needs of others? We can change the world as we lift others us. List below three specific ways your family will help the needy in your area. There are so many hurting people who need the love of Christ. What can you and your family do to change the world?

3. Are you training others to be disciplined? If you have children, describe their personalities below. How disciplined are they? After you write your description, ask God to help you train them in divine discipline.

Dear Lord,

I do want to change this hurting world. Help me to build others up through encouragement, lift them up by meeting their needs, and train them up in teaching divine discipline.

                                                              Amen

Epilogue
A Disciplined Life

There is a beautiful stone cottage in a small village in the Cotswolds of England. This lovely home is usually empty because its owner lives far away. However the caretaker goes daily to check the house and the gardener works weekly to tend the yard. The house is immaculate inside and the flowers are spectacular outside. You may ask, "Why all the work when the home is unoccupied?" I asked the same question until God revealed the answer to me. The laborers at Brookview Cottage are responsible for always having it ready for the owner, though they never know when he will come. They faithfully fulfill their duties in preparation for their master's return. The beautifully maintained cottage is evidence of their hard work and persistent discipline.

Christians have a similar responsibility: to be prepared for our Master's return. God created us for a definite purpose. While He is still the owner of our lives, He asks us to be faithful caretakers. He not only asks us to watch over our hearts and bodies, He provides the power to do it through the Holy Spirit. God tells us to persevere in our godly living and spread the gospel. We have confidence that Jesus will return one day, but we don't know when. It is our duty to be ready. How can you prepare for the Master to return? Live a life of divine discipline and share this message with others.

God has taught me so much as I have learned divine discipline. He has not only challenged me about my responsibility to be disciplined, but He has revealed to me the rewards of self-control. He has shown me areas of my life lacking in discipline and He has given me specific ways to become disciplined. He has changed me and used me to help change others. I have grown spiritually, physically, and mentally. While I have already experienced many blessings of self-discipline, I look forward to eternal rewards for my discipline and perseverance.

A few of the lessons I have learned about divine discipline are:

1. I *can* be disciplined!
2. God *will* help me in very practical ways.
3. *Others* can encourage me and I can encourage them.
4. *Freedom* is the greatest reward of self-discipline.
5. The biblical principles of self-control can apply to *all* areas of my life.
6. I must *persevere* in discipline for the rest of my life.

This Scripture inspires me to live a disciplined life: "Stand firm. Let nothing move you. Always give yourselves fully to the work of the Lord, because you know that your labor in the Lord is not in vain" (1 Corinthians 15:58). I pray that this Scripture will continue to inspire you to pursue divine discipline.

I hope you don't feel overwhelmed. Remember, Christians can claim the victory of a disciplined life because of the power of the Holy Spirit. We are helpless in our own power. But God's supernatural power can help us develop discipline in all areas of our lives. So, Christian, make a genuine commitment to develop and maintain self-control in your life. Let God help you become disciplined inwardly and outwardly.

Maybe you've tried self-discipline before and you've failed. All of us fail. Remember: lapses are the rule not the exception. Don't be discouraged. Forgive yourself and start again. That's what I did. After many failures in my own power, I have achieved many successes in God's power. We must keep on keeping on in divine discipline.

One of my dear friends has encouraged me in the writing of this book. Apparently the Lord convicted her of the lack of discipline and perseverance in her life as she proofed this manuscript. She recommitted herself to be more disciplined personally and to teach her young children to be disciplined. When school began this year, Sandra started a new practice in their home. She gets the whole family together for breakfast at seven o'clock each morning. Although it takes a lot of discipline to get up early, prepare breakfast, dress the children, and keep smiling, she knew it would be worth the personal sacrifice and morning hassle to have one meal each day as a family.

After a week of family breakfasts, Sandra asked her six-year-old daughter if she liked their new morning routine. With tears in her eyes, Sandra told me her daughter's honest response: "Yes, Mother. But you will forget." The truth of her daughter's words reminded Sandra in a painful way of her need to persevere. We all need to be more disciplined, but we especially need to persevere in a disciplined life.

My life verse has become Hebrews 12:11: "No discipline seems pleasant at the time, but painful. Later on, however, it produces a harvest of righteousness and peace for those who have been trained by it." I have read it, studied it, and memorized it. As I meditate on those words of wisdom, I remind myself that I need to practice self-control daily. Discipline is not easy or fun at first. In fact, it is difficult and painful. But when I stick with it over the long haul, discipline gives me true freedom and lasting joy. I have learned a valuable lesson — how to develop and maintain *a disciplined life*!

Dear Lord,

Thank You for teaching me
   the lesson of divine discipline.

Help me remember the worth of self-control
   and not just the rewards.

Help me discipline my life and my heart.

Give me the personal willpower
   to make a lifelong commitment.

Give me Your supernatural power
   to make lifestyle changes.

Give me the persuasive power of godly people
   to make lifechanging choices.

Help me persevere in divine discipline.

Help me practice the disciplines of life —
   spiritual, physical, and mental.

Help me use divine discipline
   to change the world.

Thank You, O Lord,
   for a disciplined life
   that is possible with You.

In Your precious name I pray.

Amen

Recommended Reading

Foster, Richard J., *Celebration of Discipline*. New York, NY: Harper & Row, 1978.

A profound book about specific disciplines of life — inward, outward, and corporate. It challenges readers to an enriched spiritual life filled with joy, peace, and a deep understanding of God.

Leavell, JoAnn P., *Don't Miss the Blessing*. Gretna, LA: Pelican Publishing Company, 1990. (Study Guide by Rhonda Harrington Kelley.)

A helpful book to promote personal and spiritual growth in Christian women, especially ministers' wives. The author looks back at past memories, around at present resources, and ahead for future blessings. The study guide is designed to encourage study of scriptures and make personal application.

Ortlund, Anne, *Disciplines of the Beautiful Woman*. Waco, TX: Word Books, 1983.

A practical guidebook for women who want to live more abundant and productive lives. Biblical principles and specific suggestions are given in the areas of attitude, appearance, schedule, organization, and goals.

Ortlund, Anne, *Disciplines of the Heart: Turning Your Inner Life to God*. Waco, TX: Word Books, 1987.

An inspirational book that concentrates on the heart and head of the Christian woman. It includes activities for individuals or groups to pursue inner spiritual growth.

Smith, Hannah Whitall, *The Christian's Secret of a Happy Life*. Waco, TX: Word Books, 1985.

Written over a hundred years ago, this powerful book confirms a life of faith not feeling. Recently reprinted with study guide by Elisabeth Elliot, it addresses the life, difficulties, and results of daily Christian living.

Willard, Dallas, *The Spirit of the Disciplines*. San Francisco, CA: Harper & Row, 1988.

A significant book on the power and purpose of spiritual disciplines. Willard explains why the disciplines work and how their practice can produce abundant life.

Notes

Chapter 1

Elliot, Elisabeth, *All That Was Ever Ours*. Old Tappan, NJ: Fleming H. Revell Company, 1988.

Foster, Richard J., *Celebration of Discipline*. New York, NY: Harper & Row, 1978.

MacDonald, Gordon, *Rebuilding Your Broken World*. Nashville, TN: Oliver Nelson, 1988.

Swindoll, Charles R., *Improving Your Serve*. Waco, TX: Word Books, 1981.

Chapter 2

Hendriksen, William, *New Testament Commentary: Exposition of Galatians*. Grand Rapids, MI: Baker Book House, 1968.

Willard, Dallas, *The Spirit of the Disciplines*. San Francisco, CA: Harper & Row, 1988.

Young, J. Terry, *The Spirit Within You*. Nashville, TN: Broadman Press, 1977.

Chapter 3

Foster, Richard J., *Celebration of Discipline*. New York, NY: Harper & Row, 1978.

MacDonald, Gail, *Keep Climbing*. Wheaton, IL: Tyndale House Publishers, 1989.

Willard, Dallas, *The Spirit of the Disciplines*. San Francisco, CA: Harper & Row, 1988.

Chapter 4

Bunyan, John, *The Pilgrim's Progress*. New York, NY: Airmont Publishing Company, Inc., 1969.

LaHaye, Tim F., *Spirit-Controlled Temperament*. Wheaton, IL: Tyndale House Publishers, 1966.

LaHaye, Tim. F., *Your Temperament: Discover Its Potential*. Wheaton: IL: Tyndale House Publishers, 1984.

Leavell, JoAnn P., *Don't Miss the Blessing*. Gretna, LA: Pelican Publishing Company, 1990.

Littauer, Florence, *Personality Plus*. Old Tappan, NJ: Fleming H. Revell Company, 1983.

MacDonald, Gordon, *Rebuilding Your Broken World*. Nashville, TN: Oliver Nelson, 1988.

Chapter 5

Holmes, Marjorie, *Secrets of Health, Energy, and Staying Young*. Garden City, NY: Doubleday & Company, 1987.

MacDonald, Gordon, *Rebuilding Your Broken World*. Nashville, TN: Oliver Nelson, 1988.

Willard, Dallas, *The Spirit of the Disciplines*. San Francisco, CA: Harper & Row, 1988.

Chapter 6

Leavell, JoAnn P., *Don't Miss the Blessing*. Gretna, LA: Pelican Publishing Company, 1990.

Ortlund, Anne, *Disciplines of the Heart: Turning Your Inner Life to God*. Dallas, TX: Word Books, 1987.

Smith, Hannah Whitall, *The Christian's Secret of a Happy Life*. Waco, TX: Word Books, 1985.

Willard, Dallas, *The Spirit of the Disciplines*. San Francisco, CA: Harper & Row, 1988.

Chapter 7

Minirth, Frank et al, *Love Hunger: Recovery from Food Addiction*.

Nashville, TN: Thomas Nelson Publishers, 1990.

Chapter 8

Leavell, JoAnn P., *Don't Miss the Blessing*. Gretna, LA: Pelican Publishing Company, 1990.

Chapter 9

Cooper, Kenneth H. and Mildred, *The New Aerobics for Women*. New York, NY: Bantam Books, 1988.

Minirth, Frank et al, *Love Hunger: Recovery from Food Addiction*. Nashville, TN: Thomas Nelson Publishers, 1990.

Swindoll, Charles R., *Starting Over*. Portland, OR: Multnomah Press, 1977.

Willard, Dallas, *The Spirit of the Disciplines*. San Francisco, CA: Harper & Row, 1988.

Chapter 10

Foster, Richard J., *Celebration of Discipline*. New York, NY: Harper & Row, 1978.

MacArthur, John F., *The MacArthur New Testament Commentary: Galatians*. Chicago, IL: Moody Press, 1987.

Smith, Hannah Whitall, *The Christian's Secret of a Happy Life*. Waco, TX: Word Books, 1985.

Chapter 11

Holmes, Marjorie, *Secrets of Health, Energy, and Staying Young*. Garden City, NY: Doubleday & Company, 1987.

Rinker, Rosalind, *Prayer: Conversing with God*. Grand Rapids, MI: Zondervan Publishing House, 1959.

Smith, Hannah Whitall, *The Christian's Secret of a Happy Life*. Waco, TX: Word Books, 1985.

Chapter 12

Anderson, Ann Kiemel, *I'm Out to Change My World*. Grand Rapids, MI: Zondervan Publishing House, 1982.

Barnes, Emilie, *Things Happen When Women Care*. Eugene, OR: Harvest House Publishers, 1990.

Holt, Pat and Ketterman, Grace, *When You Feel Like Screaming.* Wheaton, IL: Harold Shaw Publishers, 1988.

Littauer, Florence, *Silver Boxes: The Gift of Encouragement.* Dallas, TX: Word Books, 1989.

McGinn, Linda R., *Resource Guide for Women's Ministries.* Nashville, TN: Broadman Press, 1990.

Ortlund, Anne, *Discipling One Another.* Dallas, TX: Word Books, 1979.

Spradlin, Marsha, *Women of Faith in the 90's.* Birmingham, AL: New Hope, 1990.

Walters, R. P., *Counseling for Problems of Self-Control.* Waco, TX: Word Books, 1987.

Appendix A
Scriptures about Self-Control

Proverbs 12:1: whoever loves discipline, loves knowledge

Proverbs 13:18: poverty comes to one who neglects discipline

Proverbs 15:32: he who neglects discipline despises himself

Proverbs 23:12: apply your heart to discipline

Proverbs 25:28: a man who lacks self-control is like a city with walls broken down

Acts 24:25: Paul told Felix about self-control

1 Corinthians 9:25: he who competes exercises self-control

Galatians 5:22,23: the fruit of the spirit is . . . self-control

Colossians 2:5: Paul rejoiced in the discipline of the Colossian Christians

1 Timothy 3:2: the pastor ("overseer") must be self-controlled

1 Timothy 3:11: wives of deacons must be self-controlled

1 Timothy 4:7,8: discipline yourself for godliness

2 Timothy 1:7: God has given us a spirit of discipline

2 Timothy 3:2-4: in the last days, men will lack self-control

Titus 1:8: leaders ("elders") should be self-controlled

Titus 2:2: older men are to be self-controlled

Titus 2:4: older women are to train younger women to be self-controlled

Titus 2:12: we are to live self-controlled lives

Hebrews 12:7: endure hardship as discipline

Hebrews 12:8: if you lack discipline, you are like illegitimate children and not sons

Hebrews 12:11: no discipline seems pleasant at the time
2 Peter 1:5-7: add to knowledge, self-control and to self-control, perseverance

Appendix B
Nutrition and Fitness Tips

Nutrition Tips:

1. You can control what you eat.
2. Don't let anyone love you with food.
3. Eat smaller amounts, more often.
4. Learn about foods and a balanced diet.
5. Throw food away or save it for later.
6. Choose an eating place; when eating, only eat.
7. Avoid high-sodium, high-cholesterol foods.
8. Consider more than calories; nutritional content is more important.
9. Measure success by fit of clothes, not loss of pounds.
10. Healthful eating, not dieting, is the goal.

Fitness Tips:

1. There is not one best way to exercise. Find an activity that fits your interest and lifestyle.
2. Vary your type of exercise.
3. Exercise for your health, not your figure.
4. Sustained exercise for thirty minutes, three times a week is a reasonable goal.
5. Warm up before exercise; then cool down after exercise.
6. Make exercise fun and convenient.
7. Seek peer support or an exercise partner.

8. Set realistic goals; then reward your accomplishments.
9. Start!
10. Keep it up!

Appendix C
Twelve Timely Tips

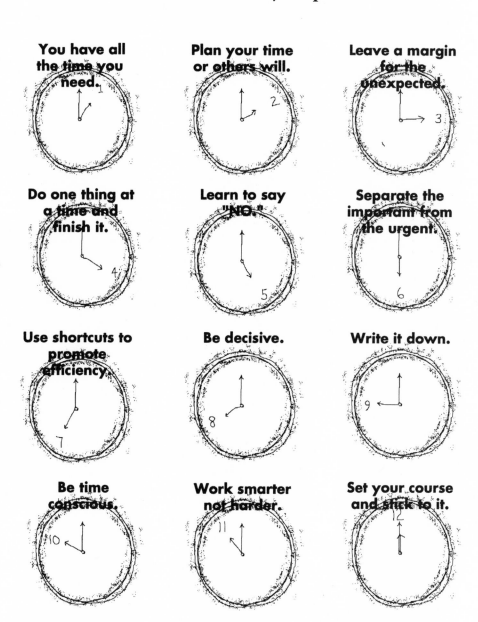

You have all the time you need.

Plan your time or others will.

Leave a margin for the unexpected.

Do one thing at a time and finish it.

Learn to say "NO."

Separate the important from the urgent.

Use shortcuts to promote efficiency.

Be decisive.

Write it down.

Be time conscious.

Work smarter not harder.

Set your course and stick to it.